Frontier of the Heart
The Search for Heroes
in Appalachia

By
Reverend Ralph W. Beiting

with
Tom Pelletier

Reverend Beiting's previous books include:

God Can Move Mountains

*Appalachia . . . a Special Place . . .
A Bridge of Hope*

Promises To Keep . . . A Vision for Appalachia

Dreams of Faith

*Called to the Mountains . . . The Autobiography
of Reverend Ralph W. Beiting*

Copies of these books can be
obtained by writing to:
Christian Appalachian Project
322 Crab Orchard Road
Lancaster, KY 40446-0001

TABLE OF CONTENTS

Dedication

There are so many people who have been heroes and heroines in my life, and to whom I owe so much. All that is good in me has come from those who raised me, taught me, guided me, supported me, and worked with me over the years.

I want to especially thank my nieces, who watch me closely and keep me in line. To each of them I give my love, and a prayer that they will continue to work on me.

This book is dedicated to my family, and to the people all over America who are opening a new frontier in the wilderness of poverty by supporting the Christian Appalachian Project.

The Christian Appalachian Project
1964-1994

More than forty years ago, Reverend Ralph W. Beiting was called to Appalachia to help ease the pain caused by poverty. In 1964, he founded an inter-denominational Christian organization called the Christian Appalachian Project (CAP). By offering long-term, self-help solutions to the problems that hold Appalachia's people back, CAP gives the poor a chance to work themselves out of poverty.

CAP provides educational programs, home repair assistance, business-development programs, and visitation programs for the elderly as well as emergency relief and more. With nearly seventy programs and activities, CAP brings hope and peace to those in need.

Through the generous work of thousands of volunteers, hundreds of local workers, and a host of loyal supporters from all over the country, CAP has become one of the largest relief organizations in America, and a pioneer in the development of programs to defeat poverty.

Prologue:
Frontier of the Heart

I am writing this book because of a man named John Findley and a campfire that took place in 1755. At that small fire, a young Daniel Boone heard a fabulous tale. John Findley, the tale's teller, and Boone were part of British Major-General Edward Braddock's mixed force of British regulars and American militia. At the beginning of the French and Indian War, this force was given the ill-fated task of marching across Pennsylvania to capture the French Fort Duquesne, at what is now Pittsburgh.

Only 20 years old, Daniel Boone gave no indication of his future as America's most famous frontiersman. He was simply a wagoner in the North Carolina regiment. As a restless soul, Daniel Boone was always fascinated by tales of adventure, and he listened to Findley with amazement.

Findley told of the fantastic land called Kentucky that lay over the Appalachian Mountains. He told Daniel of the wild game whose abundance could hardly be imagined. He told him of the beauty of the mountains and rivers and forests. He courted Boone's imagination with the opportunities that waited for a man with courage. I am sure Daniel Boone must have dreamt that night of the magical land of Kentucky.

Before Braddock reached Duquesne, his doomed army was ambushed and scores of men died, including the General himself, but Daniel Boone survived, and the flame of inspiration that John Findley lit in his heart burned the rest of his life.

As a young boy, I loved to read of Daniel Boone's adventures. By 1950, I was walking where he had walked, and living where he had lived, and that was no small coincidence. Throughout my life, Daniel Boone has been my hero.

But as I sit down to write my sixth book for the many wonderful supporters, volunteers, and employees of the Christian Appalachian Project (CAP), I find myself comparing my role to that of John Findley more than Daniel Boone. I no longer have the youthful strength and energy to walk the long trails and climb the mountains as Boone did. But I hope I can still tell a story, and I hope I can still inspire the hearts of men and women about the potential of this land over the mountains.

I hope I can still paint a vision that will lure those who yearn to do something exciting and meaningful. I hope I can call them to create a new frontier—a frontier of the heart—out of the wilderness of poverty and despair in Appalachia.

In my last book, I told you about my life and about the things that inspired me and guided me in my journey. In this book, I want to talk about the men and women who came before me in Appalachia. I hope that by telling a little about my heroes, I can show why I care so much about this region, and I hope their stories will inspire you to become a hero in your own life.

Not all of Appalachia's history is inspiring, of course. In particular, it is tragic that so much bloodshed occurred between the white pioneers and the Native Americans who lived and hunted first in the lands beyond the Appalachians. I wish they could have shared a land that by all accounts was bountiful enough for all.

My heroes were not perfect. They, like you and me, carried their treasures in earthen vessels. These were ordinary people who, with courage and determination, did extraordinary things and helped build the trail to the West that inspired Americans for more than a century. The problems they faced and the dangers they endured are different from those that confront us today. But the challenge they faced is, in a very real sense, the same one that remains for us. "Can we cross the mountains? Can we endure? Can we explore a new frontier of the heart and build something lasting?"

It is fitting that as I begin this book about the heroes of Appalachia, my mind turns to John

Findley. Findley was one of the very first frontiersmen ever to see the land of Kentucky. He joined a party of explorers who floated down the Ohio River to Kentucky. He hunted, he traveled, he traded with the Native Americans, and he dreamed. On that trip he learned of an overland route to Kentucky through a gap in the imposing mountains. That gap would one day be famous — the Cumberland Gap. At that time, however, few people knew of the gap, and fewer still knew how to find it.

When John Findley huddled with Daniel Boone over the warmth of a log fire, he told Daniel about the mythical Cumberland Gap, the gateway to the glorious land of Kentucky. In many ways, I see my own role today as very similar. I know there is a path to this new frontier of the heart that could bring many people adventure and fulfillment. It is not an easy path to find, and it doesn't lead to riches, but to something far more important — a sense of worthwhile achievement that is harder to find than wealth.

John Findley recognized in Daniel Boone the potential of a great explorer and builder. In writing this book I hope I can reach the explorer and builder in everyone who reads it. Whether you come to volunteer and work in the mountains with us, send donations from afar to help us build the new frontier, pray for our work, or help in some other way, I hope I can show you that what we are doing here is of historic, lasting importance, and to play a part is an adventure in and of itself.

I must admit that as I enter my seventies, I wonder if I am too old to continue my part in this mission called the Christian Appalachian Project. I wonder if I am too tired to be inspirational. But then I think about John Findley and his effect on Daniel Boone. The truth is that after those campfire tales in 1755, Daniel Boone did not immediately set out to explore Kentucky. When Braddock's army broke up, Findley and Boone lost track of each other. Daniel Boone returned to his home, married Rebecca Bryan and settled down to farm and raise a family. The spark that John Findley ignited still glowed in his heart, but it did not yet urge him to action.

Then one day, nearly fourteen years after that campfire, a man leading a pack-horse stopped at the Boone farm. Whether he remembered Boone and was searching for him, or whether it was simply luck that he found him again, will never be known, but the man was none other than John Findley. Once again, this time over the warm fire in the Boones' cabin, John Findley spun his yarn. He told Daniel he had been back to Kentucky and it was even better than he'd first thought. "Kaintuck'," he said, "There was a land for you. Game in such abundance as no man dreamed of. A deer at every lick. Buffalo thick upon the traces. Buffalo herds so huge that a man had to be careful lest he be crushed to death in their mad stampedes. The ground rumbling with their hoofs. At the falls of the Ohio, wild geese and ducks so plentiful there was no need even to kill them. All a man could eat were drawn by the current over the falls and thrown up freshly killed on the banks below. One might pick up enough fresh fowl for dinner any day. And land—land such as a man might dream of. Well watered, lush and green, with fertile soil in all directions."[1]

This time Findley's tale was irresistible, and when he left, Daniel Boone was never the same. He knew he had to cross the mountains and lead people to a new home. He could never be ordinary again. He could no longer live a safe life. Now he had to climb the mountains. He had to cross the streams. He had to explore wild places and bring people with him to make a new home in the wilderness beyond.

Sometimes I ask myself, "What if John Findley had not found Daniel Boone the second time? What if his tale had only inspired fear of the dangers and lack of confidence in the chances for success?" It's quite possible that the land west of the Appalachian Mountains would still be British or French, and the United States of America would

---

1. *Daniel Boone, Master of the Wilderness*, John Bakeless, University of Nebraska Press, 1989, page 44–45.

still be just the thirteen eastern colonies.

That's why I can't quit yet. That's why I have to write this book in the hopes of lighting fires in the hearts of those with an adventuring spirit. That's why I must keep telling the tale of Appalachia and the great potential that still lies undiscovered here.

In the chapters ahead, I hope to do that by relating stories of the great heroes and pioneers who first built this land. I hope to show how they faced and solved problems, and how the people of Appalachia today, with the help of the Christian Appalachian Project, are trying to face and solve their problems with the same virtues.

It took heroes to brave the dangers of the frontier in the old days, and it will take heroes to revive Appalachia today. The heroes are here, and they are all across this country—I know they are. Maybe you are one of them.

I pray that like the heroes of old, you and I can add a new page to the story of America—and together open our hearts to create a new frontier for Appalachia . . . a frontier of the heart.

Heroes and Dreamers

Of all the insults in the world, I've always loved to be called a "foolish dreamer." The foolish dreamers of the world are my heroes. I think that's why I have always been so fascinated by those foolish dreamers—the early Appalachian pioneers. Of them all, the most heroic dreamer was Daniel Boone.

After John Findley's second inspirational talk, Daniel could no longer hold his dream inside. Setting out in the spring of 1769 with Findley, Daniel's best friend John Stuart, and three other brave men, Boone crossed the mountains into Kentucky and began hunting and exploring. All that Findley had told him about Kentucky was true. It was a beautiful land filled with game, and broad plains that would one day make rich farmland. The spark of Boone's dream was now fanned into a blazing bonfire. Exploring this new land and starting a new home with his family was all Daniel could think about.

It was like this for many of those first pioneers. Their dreams dominated their lives and drove them to remarkable achievements against great odds and dangers.

The thing that saddens me most about Appalachia today is that the spirit of those dreamers who first settled these mountains and valleys has been squashed by poverty, despair, and the decline of spiritual life.

When the human imagination is deprived of dreams, it creates nightmares. Some time ago, a young woman named Sally, a Christian Appalachian Project volunteer, assembled a group of youngsters at one of our teen centers. CAP operates these centers in the poorest areas of Appalachia to provide alternatives to idleness and alcohol and drug abuse for young people. Sally asked the teens at the center to draw pictures of the future. One by one they created their visions. They drew garbage, cities covered in pollution, a landscape devoid of trees. They drew hypodermic needles, fires, and nuclear holocausts. Without exception, every image was frightening.

What a sharp contrast these nightmares are to the pictures John Findley painted of the future for Daniel Boone. Could Boone have done the remarkable things he did with nightmares of the future, instead of dreams? I don't think so.

No, it was a wonderful dream of the future that drove Daniel on. After reaching Kentucky, he and his band continued to explore for more than a year. Over time, danger and fear took its toll. Daniel's best friend, John Stuart, disappeared and was never seen again. Eventually, the other men returned to the safety of the "settlements."

Finally, Boone was completely alone, quite possibly the only pioneer in all of Kentucky. He had not seen his wife or children in more than a year. He later told how he sat alone in his small camp and became depressed. For a moment, he considered giving up his dream.

Luckily, Daniel refused to give in to his brief brush with melancholy. Instead he followed the dream. Exploring by himself, he pushed further into the wilds of Kentucky than he had ever been before. He was constantly aware of the danger from wild animals and other risks. But he was not afraid. He later explained why he thought a man tormented by fear was an unhappy man. He said if danger doesn't come, fear is only wasted energy. And if danger does come, fear only gets in the way of effective action.

Finally, after exploring the area completely and satisfying himself that Kentucky was the land of his dreams, Daniel returned home to North Carolina. He had been in the wilderness for nearly two years. He knew the wilds of Kentucky better than anyone in the thirteen Colonies. And he was prepared to lead the founding of a whole new colony in Kentucky.

What could have enticed Daniel Boone to leave the security of his small farm in Carolina? What made him brave when everyone else had given in to fear? I think he was consumed by a dream. He could sooner fly than ignore that dream, or let fear stand in its way.

He was certainly a "foolish dreamer."

I think this is true of all the people down through history whom we revere as heroes. Daniel Boone was, by all accounts, a happy man, but he was never satisfied. There was always another mountain to climb and another wilderness to explore.

Through the power of his dreams, and his courage in forsaking all safety to follow them, he attracted first tens, then hundreds, and finally thousands of people to follow their own dreams with him to a new country.

I wish we had more heroic dreamers these days—in Appalachia and in the rest of America. Today, we seem to have a great craving for security. We want to be safe. But true security doesn't come from standing still. The Almighty has instilled in each of us an urge to explore. We have to discover and create. That is what makes us the free men and women of our time.

That's why, more and more these days, I try to help the people of Appalachia remember how to dream.

I hesitate to compare myself to such a great dreamer as Daniel Boone, but I feel that my own life has been one of following a dream. When I first came to Appalachia and felt the depths of the despair of people trapped in poverty, I dreamed that I could make a difference to a few people. Later my dream grew and I hoped that many people would step forward and that we could help all the people of Appalachia.

Today as I walk the paths and creeks that Daniel Boone once walked, I try to revive the spirit of adventure, of risk taking.

This past spring, CAP helped start a bakery, which makes breakfast biscuits and other finger snacks, in an area with little employment outside of the declining coal mines. Many people have told me that the project is doomed to failure, just as Daniel Boone's neighbors probably told him that his dream of settling in Kentucky was doomed to failure. I don't know how this bakery will turn out. Maybe the naysayers are right. But at CAP, we think there's a real chance to create good jobs for 60 or 100 people—and we're not afraid to take a chance.

I am also trying to start a furniture industry here. In these mountains we have some of the largest hardwood forests left in America. Unfortunately, most of it is cut and shipped off to distant cities for processing into furniture. This provides a few, mostly low-paying jobs cutting the timber. Why can't we build the furniture right here, at the source of the wood, and create a new industry with good jobs? That would be exciting, and I can't help but keep dreaming about it.

Recently I gave an invocation at the ground-breaking of the new Kentucky Rural Economic Development Center in eastern Kentucky that will help create jobs, improve our education, develop our agriculture, and bring tourism to Appalachia. As I stood on the platform and heard congressmen and other dignitaries speak of the potential of this new dream, I was terribly proud. There's nothing I love more than sharing in a dream.

More than anything, I want to help make sure the next generation of children in Appalachia knows how to dream. Because of isolation and the feelings of helplessness and hopelessness that poverty creates, many parents in Appalachia discourage their children from dreaming. "The world is dangerous," they say. Worse yet, they say, "Why bother with school or college? There's nothing out there for you anyway. Just stay here and do as your daddy or your mommy did."

When I speak to children in our child development centers, teen centers, and summer camps, I say, "Let's take a chance. Let's create something new." I say, "Stay in school. Go to college." When the children ask "Why?" I don't give the usual answer, "To get a good job." To me, that's too small a dream. I say to them, "To change the world."

I love the way fire burns in their eyes when I say that.

I believe that fire comes from God. As much

as I admire Daniel Boone's courage and his power as a dreamer, there is one whose example as a hero and a dreamer has inspired me even more. We know Him as Jesus of Nazareth.

He was probably the world's greatest pioneer and dreamer. He was living a quiet, safe life as a carpenter in Nazareth when He decided to leave it all behind. From the day that He met John the Baptist in the River Jordan and started on His journey to Calvary, He excited the world as no man has ever done before or since. Like Daniel Boone, He inspired others to follow Him and dream new, bigger dreams. When Jesus chose John and Andrew as His disciples, they said, "If we come with you, where will we live?" I can imagine Daniel Boone's fellow pioneers saying the same thing to him. Jesus said "Follow me and you will see."

To Peter, Andrew, James, and John, the prosperous fishermen, He said "Put your nets aside. Leave your boats on shore. Come, follow me and I will make you fishers of men."

At the end of His ministry on earth, Jesus again challenged His disciples to follow Him. He told them "Go forth into the whole world and preach the Good News to every creature."

Like the pioneers who followed Daniel Boone into the wilderness of Kentucky, the men and women who followed Jesus into the spiritual wilderness must have asked, "How will we know what to do?'' I can picture Daniel Boone standing at the mouth of the Cumberland Gap saying, ''Don't worry, I'll be with you and I know what I'm doing.''

Jesus said the same thing to His disciples 2000 years ago, and He says it to us today. ''Don't worry. I will never leave you orphans. I will always be with you, walking beside you in all your trials.''

What a dreamer! He never told His disciples that their lives would be easy or safe. In fact, He said just the opposite. Yet they followed Him, and billions of people have followed Him since that day. That is the power of a dream.

Daniel Boone left his family and risked everything he owned to go off into the wilderness. By risking everything, he won something of great value. He learned the wilds of Kentucky backwards and forwards so that when the courage of the pioneers wavered, they found faith in his knowledge of the trails and rivers and the ways of the woods. Through him they found the strength to go on.

When Jesus left everything behind, even life, He won something of great spiritual value. When we falter in our dreams; when we grow fearful of the dark and the wilds of this life, we can find faith in His knowledge of us and the ways of our hearts. And we can find the strength to go on.

Nowhere do we need that strength more than

in modern Appalachia. When John Findley swayed Daniel Boone's heart, he described this as a land of unbelievable opportunity. Now it too often seems to be a land of broken dreams.

After 44 years of trying to inspire people to dream and take risks, I feel a new day dawning. More and more I hear young people talk about their dreams.

A few weeks after Sally, the volunteer at our teen center, asked that group of young people to draw their visions of the future, she asked the same group to take part in a small dream. She gathered them on a Saturday and took them to the house of a wonderful old woman named Frances, whom Sally had visited as part of our Elderly Visitation program. Frances lived in a shack back in one of the hollers of Appalachia. She had lived a long, difficult, but happy life in the mountains, but in her old age and solitude many everyday tasks had become too difficult for her.

The teens spent the day clearing Frances' yard, cleaning her coal stove, and sprucing up the humble house. That evening they were tired but happy, bubbling over with enthusiasm for the good deed they had done and the new friend they had made.

Many of them continued to visit Frances, fixing up her house, bringing in her firewood, and brightening her days with their joy and their company. When Frances passed away recently, the teens were saddened, but proud that they had helped make her last months easier and happier.

It was a small dream, to take a bunch of disadvantaged teenagers and show them that they could help someone else — and find joy in the process. But it was a good dream, and one that has changed the lives of some good kids. Who knows, maybe the next time they imagine the future, they'll draw pictures of people helping one another, learning and sharing together.

There is power in every dream, no matter how small. That's why I hope and pray that you will nourish dreams in your own life, and dream with me of a new frontier in Appalachia. We need all the foolish dreamers we can get.

Heroes of Courage

Daniel Boone may not have known fear, but most of us live with fear every day. I know I do. Fear of failure, fear of rejection, fear of growing old. I could go on and on. Not many can live without fear, but all of us can live a life of courage. To me, courage is not the absence of fear, but the determination to overcome fear and choose the dark, difficult trail that leads to our dreams. One of my favorite heroes of courage is Dr. Thomas Walker.

Though he was a doctor and was, at the age of 35, already quite well off, Thomas Walker decided he didn't want an easy life. What he really wanted was to explore where no one else had been. So in 1750, young Dr. Walker watched safety and civilization slip behind him.

With five other men, he set out to find land for the Loyal Land Company. As he and his band passed through Virginia towards the looming barrier of the Appalachian Mountains, settlements became more and more sparse. Towns gave way to small clusters of cabins, which gave way to isolated farms, until finally the men were completely alone in a vast uncharted forest.

I think about how those men must have felt as they left all that was familiar and safe far behind. They must have been worried—if not downright terrified. Bears attacked their dogs. Danger lurked around every tree. The unknown lay everywhere like a thick mist.

Yet, inspired by Dr. Walker's leadership and courage, the men continued in the face of great danger, and in spite of their fears. And on April 13, 1750, they made a discovery that was to change the course of American history and open a new frontier. From Dr. Walker's notebook of the journey it's not clear that he grasped the significance of what he had found. He describes passing through a gap in the imposing mountains and heading down into what is now Kentucky. He came upon the headwaters of a river which he named the Cumberland River in honor of the Duke of Cumberland. Later that name would be applied to the pass he had discovered through the mountains—a pass that every grade school student knows as "The Cumberland Gap."

It might have been more fitting and more descriptive if it were called "The Walker Gap," because it was Dr. Walker's courage that opened up this gateway through the mountains through which so many pioneers would cross into a new future.

I find Thomas Walker's story inspiring for us in Appalachia today. It's a story of extreme courage to leave the safe and sure, and venture into the unknown.

If I could convince more of Appalachia's people to imitate Dr. Walker, we could make a greater dent in the poverty and despair of this area. We need courage to abandon old ways and forge new ones. We need courage to develop break-through ideas that can lead us to a new frontier.

Nowhere is that courage needed more than in the dream of economic development for this area. For generations, coal was practically the only source of income in the mountains. Dr. Walker himself may have helped start the coal industry that was our ace-in-the-hole for so long. In the journals of his fateful trip, he mentions finding coal in the mountains. He was probably one of the first to note this resource that once sustained the economy of Appalachia.

But now the coal is dwindling and competition from oil has lowered the price so much that exploration for new coal veins has all but ended.

That's why we need to find new economic opportunities for the people of Appalachia. We need industries that will give Appalachia a chance to contribute to America's economy. So many people I meet are desperately in need of a livelihood of which they can be proud. Too many are trapped on welfare and afraid to get off. The few available jobs are minimum wage and part-time. Many families are better off financially if they do nothing and remain on welfare.

There is also a feeling among many people who live in isolated areas of the mountains that the outside world is too scary to face. The other day I was talking to a young boy who told me "My daddy says don't trust nobody." I was sad to hear that.

You see how much we need courage? We need people to heed the example of Dr. Walker and leave the safety of the old ways of coal and welfare and set out into a new world.

We must instill in our youth a sense of adventure and courage early on. When we bring children to CAP's summer camps and Bible Schools, we don't do it just for the fun, although many of these kids sorely need that. I hope that exposing the children to new ideas and dreams and to the idealism and courage of our volunteers, will awaken their natural courage. We tell the kids, "Start dreaming. Don't let people tell you you shouldn't take chances, or you can't trust others. Have faith. Have confidence. Have courage."

We also try very hard to convince their parents to have courage. Often when I talk to illiterate adults, they tell me, "Reverend, I'm too old to learn to read. People will laugh at me. I just couldn't stand it." So they continue to barely survive, with no real chance for change.

Change comes only with courage. If Dr. Walker had given in to his fears of the unknown and stayed in Fredericksburg, Virginia, exploration of the land beyond the mountains might have been set back a generation.

I am terribly proud of those people who find the courage to make dramatic changes—even when it would be easier to continue as they are. Bonnie is one of those people.

As a child in Rockcastle County, Kentucky, Bonnie took a terrible fall while ice skating. She broke her collarbone, a hip, both jawbones, and several ribs. But there was another, far more serious injury. Bonnie hit her head so hard that she was in a coma for three days. When she woke up, she discovered she no longer knew how to read. Bonnie went back to school six months after her accident, but she says, ''It was like starting from the first grade again.''

Education in Appalachia, even today, is a tenuous opportunity. The kids start from so far behind that any small problem can doom them to failure. And Bonnie's problem was a big one.

She tried very hard to catch up again, but realized she couldn't and eventually dropped out. Then, like so many young, uneducated girls in Appalachia, she exercised her only other option. She got married at a very young age.

Bonnie doesn't regret the nine wonderful children she raised, or that she raised them in a home without electricity or running water. But all her life she dreamed that one day she'd be able to read again. Three years ago, with the help of CAP and our supporters, Bonnie found the courage to take the first steps towards her own Cumberland Gap. She came to CAP's Adult Learning Center and said, "I want to learn to read better." She's been going to classes ever since.

She has progressed steadily, starting at a third or fourth grade level, and by the time this book is published, she'll probably have gained her high school equivalency diploma. Her dedication and courage are so inspiring that nearby Berea College is interested in talking to her about a full scholarship.

But there's even more to Bonnie's story. Like the Dr. Walkers of the pioneer days, Bonnie wants to lead others through the Cumberland Gap to a new world of opportunity. She goes to local schools and community groups and gives inspiring talks about the importance of literacy. She volunteers at our Adult Learning Center, helping others find the road to reading. Last fall she was even chosen as one of three Kentucky representatives to the National New Readers Congress in Washington, D.C.

By following her dream with tremendous courage, Bonnie is changing the world.

It may seem like a small change right now, but remember, when Dr. Walker hiked over the

Cumberland Gap, he had no idea where it would lead. That's what happens when we have courage.

Sometimes I find the small displays of courage most inspiring. Because of poor health care and other results of poverty, we have many disabled people in Appalachia. CAPRICE (Christian Appalachian Project Resources for Independence and Community Employment) helps people with disabilities move steadily towards their full potential. Every step they take is a victory of courage. To me, they are all heroes of courage.

The other day I took a group of adults with disabilities for an outing on a houseboat. They enjoy this opportunity to break the routine and do something different.

Usually, I surprise them by asking if anyone would like to drive the boat. It's a fairly large boat, about 60 feet long and 16 feet wide, and the idea of driving it is quite intimidating to most people, disabled or not. Usually they say, "No way. I could never do that." But I say, "Come on, give it a try and we'll help each other."

Before long, someone with courage will step up and take the wheel. His or her example will inspire others and pretty soon many of the people are taking a turn—and overcoming their fear with a little bit of courage.

On this one trip, after several people had taken a turn driving, a man with dwarfism approached me. He said, "I would like to drive. Can you help me get up into the chair?''

That must have taken a lot of courage, both to overcome the fear of driving the boat and also to overcome his embarrassment about not being able to reach the chair himself. But within a short time he had the whole operation down pat. He drove around the lake for half an hour, enjoying every minute. Later, he told me he'd like to become a boat driver. It's a small dream, maybe, but one that will take a lot of courage for him to reach. After watching him that day, I have no doubt he has that kind of courage.

We all do, deep down inside.

Courage is one of God's greatest gifts to humanity. He knows we live in a difficult world, so He gave us the courage to overcome our fears.

Jesus constantly called the Apostles to be brave. We all know the story of the mighty storm that arose when He sailed with His new disciples on their fishing boat. The sea was so violent that the disciples feared for their lives. They tried every trick they knew to protect their boat from capsizing, still the waves threatened. Finally, in desperation, they woke Jesus and told Him, ''We are going to drown!''

Jesus said, ''Oh you of little faith, why did you doubt? Where is your faith? I am with you.''

That faith, that God is always with us, should constantly feed our courage. Why should we be afraid when the Lord is with us?

On another occasion, thousands of people gathered to see Jesus and hear Him preach. As evening drew near, the Apostles told Him, "Master, this is a deserted place and it is already late; dismiss the crowds so that they can go to the villages and buy food for themselves." I'm sure the Apostles were afraid of the large and probably unruly crowd. They must have worried that the hungry crowd could turn angry.

But Jesus told the Apostles to do the best they could. "Don't be afraid. Give them whatever you have and leave the rest up to me."

We all know the result: the miracle of how five thousand people were fed with five loaves and two fish—with twelve baskets left over.

All God asks is that we have the courage to try. He'll take care of the rest.

This is an important lesson for us in Appalachia, as well as the rest of America. America has so many problems now, but we seem to be afraid to face them. People say, "Let's not rock the boat. Let's live with the demons we know and not risk awakening demons we don't yet know."

We all dream of a better world, but without courage those dreams are useless. Even worse, they are like a drug that makes you feel better for a few minutes but ruins your life in the process. To be people of dreams, we must have courage. Without it we can't make changes and we might as well give up today.

Having courage is not easy. I would never, ever pretend that it is. But as Jesus said, "Enter through the narrow gate; for the gate is wide and the road broad that leads to destruction . . . How narrow the gate and constricted the road that leads to life."

I wonder if Thomas Walker recalled that passage from the Gospel of Matthew as he moved through the Cumberland Gap and became the first European to see the land of Kentucky?

He was far from the last, of course. First he was followed by a few brave souls like Daniel Boone, then more and more, until the people were passing over the mountains in waves, heading west to a new frontier that eventually extended all the way to the Pacific.

One of the things I hope most about my own life is that I have lived with courage, and infected others with that courage. I was heartened last week when I spoke with the schoolteacher of the little boy who told me his daddy warned him "Don't trust nobody." She told me the little boy had to write a paper about what he wanted to be when he grew up. He wrote "I want to work with Reverend Beiting to help make the world better."

They say that fear is contagious. Well, so is courage.

Heroes of Generosity

I have always wondered why Daniel Boone didn't just stake his claim to a large plot of land in Kentucky, build a plantation, and grow rich. He certainly could have. As one of the first to explore the land, he knew where the choice parcels lay.

Yet he knew hundreds of families back in the Colonies wanted that same opportunity to build a new world. He spent most of his life helping them reach their dreams. It was not an easy sacrifice for him to make. If he had paid more attention to his own property and less to helping others, he might have become wealthy. As it was, at the end of his life, Boone was nearly penniless, but he never counted that loss with bitterness towards the people he helped. One day, in the fall of 1773, he showed his complete generosity to others.

Boone assembled a group of 30 pioneers who wanted to cross the mountains and settle in the new land of Kentucky. When the group inventoried the supplies they needed to survive the winter before

they could grow new crops, they were short on
flour and farming tools. Daniel sent his oldest son,
James, back for additional supplies. It was the last
time Daniel saw his son alive.

After securing the supplies, James and a group
of four or five men hurried to catch up with the
main party of settlers. One night, unaware that
they were only about three miles behind, they
stopped to make camp. That night they were
attacked and killed by a group of Cherokees who
may have been angry at the encroachment of
settlers onto their hunting grounds. The next day,
a man from the settlers' main camp found the scene
of James' death and alerted the rest of the group.

As Daniel Boone hastily buried his son, the
settlers panicked. Even Boone's authority and
reassurance could not convince them to continue
the trip. In the end, Daniel had no choice but to
lead them back home.

The loss of his son weighed heavily on his heart,
and in May of the following year, he went back
alone to James' grave. He found the spot, and saw
that wolves had been digging at the grave. He un-
covered the decomposed body and rewrapped it
in a cloth. Then he dug a deeper hole and buried
it properly and covered it with stones so the
animals could no longer disturb it.

He sat alone under the tree that sheltered the
grave. It was the worst day of his life. He later
wrote, ''James was a good son and I looked

forward to a long and useful life for him, but it was not to be.'' These simple words could not begin to describe the pain he felt. The loss of his first-born son was one he would never get over.

Yet he continued to lead others over the mountains and into the new land. He gave of himself constantly to help others follow their dreams. To me, that marks him as a great hero of generosity. That's no small distinction.

Daniel Boone was not the only hero of generosity in Appalachia. Generosity and sharing were a way of life—maybe the only way of life. The pioneers were living so much on the edge of life that survival without the help of friends was nearly impossible. The generosity of one pioneer would likely be repaid by another down the line.

Even in the face of great poverty, that generous spirit lives on in Appalachia today. I often meet with families who have virtually nothing in the world. As I sit in their homes it's hard not to notice that the houses are practically falling down around me. Yet, they nearly always have something they want to share with me. Sometimes it's a ripe tomato from the backyard garden. Sometimes it's something a family member has carved out of wood.

The generous spirit is certainly not limited to Appalachia. Generosity is one of the most basic human traits—a reflection of God. We need to encourage this wonderful characteristic and give it opportunities to grow and create.

I am deeply moved by the many donations, large and small, that CAP receives from people all over the country. Often, these donations represent a real sacrifice from people who have little themselves. When I see the tremendous love that flows in with these donations, I am both awed and humbled.

I meet the people in need here in Appalachia every day. I cannot help but be moved to help. But the people who send donations from afar are making a sacrifice for people they have never even met. That's real generosity. To me, all our supporters are heroes of generosity. They light a candle in the darkness of greed that seems to have engulfed this country. One of the ways that our donors' generosity reaches out to the people of the mountains is through our Christmas Basket program.

By providing gifts to poverty-stricken families at Christmas, we celebrate the greatest gift of all: God's gift of His only Son.

With the help of generous friends who sponsor one or more families, we begin assembling baskets in September, and include warm clothing, good food, and books. When there are children, we add toys. Our Christmas Baskets won't end poverty, or even make a dent in the deprivation of these families, but they bring a sense of joy and sharing that goes far beyond the value of the items. It reminds the people of the mountains that they aren't alone. There are friends all over the country who care about them, and who are willing to sacrifice to help them reach their dreams. In connection with our Christmas Basket program, we have a community Christmas service where we sing carols, read the Bible, and pray. In the following days we hand out the Christmas Baskets to the needy. At one of these services, we invited a wonderful woman named Maura to talk about her long life and what Christmas meant to her. It wasn't easy for Maura because her husband died on Christmas Day seven years ago. But she was looking forward to telling everyone of her love for Christ and her hope for the future.

I find the faith of people like Maura amazing. Maura was 84 years old. She suffered from diabetes and Hodgkins disease and since the death of her husband, she lived alone without help, in a house that was barely habitable. The floors were so bad that they had fallen through to the ground in many places. Her bedroom looked like a rolling sea and Maura was afraid to sleep there because the floor might give way completely some night. So instead she took her rest on the old sofa in the living room.

Yet, rather than be bitter about her fate, Maura was grateful that she could still be independent and could still live at home, humble though it was. And she was always extremely grateful whenever we visited her to see how she was getting on.

We looked forward to Maura's talk at our Christmas service, but unfortunately, she became very ill at the last minute and couldn't make it. The service went on without her, but it wasn't quite the same. During the service, the children decorated a very special Christmas tree with ornaments they had made by hand. It was beautiful—and we knew just what to do with it. When the service was over, several people gathered up that tree, packed it in a car, and drove the back roads to Maura's house. She gasped when she opened her front door and saw the tree. She hadn't had a Christmas tree since her husband died. When the tree was in her living room, with lights twinkling, she cried tears of joy and said "This is the best Christmas I've ever had."

This is what generosity can do. Is it worth it? The gratitude and love in Maura's eyes gave me all the answer I'll ever need. (By the way, through our Home Repair Program, we built Maura a new little house. Now she can sleep safely in her own bedroom again.)

Generosity is a marvelous force. I'm always amazed at how it multiplies. That's why I insist that CAP help other groups doing good work in Appalachia. By supporting other charitable groups we can aid more people than we ever could by ourselves. And we help generosity and community blossom in the mountains.

I know from experience that when you are

generous yourself, you get what you need in return.

Recently I loaned some money to a local company that employs 60 people. I only had part of the money I had promised, but the company was in serious trouble and I hated to see those jobs lost. I wondered where I would get the rest of the funds.

That morning at Mass I asked God for help. When I got into my car to return home, I saw an envelope on the seat. Inside was a check from a wonderful friend to cover the exact amount I needed.

I don't know how this works. It doesn't make any sense. But I have faith. I'm convinced that God controls this repayment of generosity, making sure that generosity does not go unrewarded. It must be one of His most fun jobs.

Jesus told us it would be like this. One day Peter came to Him with a troubled heart. Peter was a successful fisherman. He said to Jesus, "Lord, we have given up our businesses, we've given up our families and friends, and we have wandered about, following you. But we are wondering, what reward are we going to get for all this?" Jesus told him, "Whatever you give up for me, you will receive on this earth a hundred times as much. And in the world that is to come you will receive everlasting joy."

Where else can you get a return like that?

Generosity is the key to renewal in Appalachia. America owes a great debt to those first Appalachian heroes of generosity. Without them, this country would not be what it is today. Today, the pendulum has swung the other way, and Appalachia must rely on the wonderful generosity of friends all over America who donate to help the poor in the mountains. But the pendulum will swing once more. I'm sure of that. Someday soon, Appalachia will repay all the heroes of generosity who have helped her open a new frontier.

Heroes of Wisdom

If I could be a hero, I'd want to be a hero of wisdom. We probably need such heroes more than anything else. They're the ones who lead us through difficult and changing times.

The early days of the Kentucky settlements certainly were such a time. And if it wasn't for what I consider to be a tremendously wise and foresighted decision made at that time, the United States of America might not be what it is today.

In early 1775, Colonel Richard Henderson, a Virginia judge, and his partners, formed a company called the Transylvania Company to secure land in Kentucky. At Sycamore Shoals, Tennessee, they met with the leaders of the Cherokee nation to strike a deal. They convinced the Cherokees to sell their hunting grounds, and signed a treaty giving the Transylvania Company possession of 20 million acres—most of what is now Kentucky.

Henderson wasted no time in finding settlers for this new land, and he hired Daniel Boone to lead a group of pioneers to create the settlement called Boonesborough. At first, Henderson's plan was to make money by selling land, and through his Transylvania Company, collect a perpetual yearly rent on every acre from the settlers.

But as it looked more and more certain that the colonies would split from England, Henderson's ambitions grew. He threatened to separate Kentucky from the other colonies and form an entirely new country called Transylvania.

Henderson's extreme ambitions combined with his dictatorial nature turned many Kentucky settlers against him. The growing settlements of Harrodsburg and Logan's Station sent a delegation to Virginia to convince the legislature to thwart Henderson's plans for an empire by declaring Kentucky a county of Virginia.

Luckily, Virginia leaders like Thomas Jefferson and Patrick Henry saw the wisdom in this suggestion. They insisted on Virginia's prior claim to the land Henderson called Transylvania. They also objected to Henderson's use of perpetual rents on land. They felt this was a continuation of the kind of economic slavery from which the colonies were trying to win independence. All through that tumultuous year of 1775, the issue was debated in the Virginia legislature, and finally, in November of 1775, Virginia reasserted its claims over Kentucky and abolished the Transylvania Company. Colonel Henderson was eventually given another large tract of land in reward for his very real contributions to settlement in Kentucky, but

Kentucky became a county of Virginia and Transylvania was dead.

Thomas Jefferson, Patrick Henry, and the other members of the Virginia legislature showed great wisdom in this decision. The truth is that Kentucky was not their biggest concern at the time. Virginia was preoccupied with the great debate over independence from England. The Transylvania issue must have struck the legislators as a nuisance. Yet rather than pass it over, they took the time to make a long-range decision that ensured that the new United States had room to grow westward. And less than twenty years later, Kentucky became the 15th state.

The wisdom of those men in Virginia helped create a sense of belonging and unity that has meant a lot to the people of Kentucky. It's no accident that our state motto is "United We Stand, Divided We Fall."

Unity is often a very wise thing, but wisdom also means knowing when to stand apart. I am very proud that some Kentuckians, for example, were among the first to call for the abolition of slavery. They recognized the wise words that Thomas Jefferson wrote in the Declaration of Independence, "All men are created equal," must apply to men and women of all races.

As a young man, Reverend David Barrow believed in the wisdom that freedom belonged to all. After fighting in the Revolutionary War, he began to preach in Virginia about the evil of slavery. It was not a popular stand at the time, and he was persecuted by his neighbors. He moved to Kentucky and continued his fight to end slavery. It was equally unpopular in Kentucky, and eventually the establishment in his Baptist church association became fed up with his anti-slavery activities and expelled him. He started his own association of anti-slavery Baptist churches leading to the formation of the Kentucky Abolition Society, which published one of the first anti-slavery magazines in America in 1808.

Most people in Kentucky were strongly pro-slavery. But Reverend Barrow and his followers had the courage and wisdom to stand apart and disagree. Others argued that the agricultural economy of Kentucky depended on slavery. But Reverend Barrow had the wisdom to say slavery was wrong, no matter what the economics.

Though he died in 1819 and didn't live to see the abolition of slavery at the end of the Civil War, his courage and wisdom played an important role that went far beyond his own congregation.

In fact, one of the members of his anti-slavery church association was Thomas Lincoln, father of Abraham Lincoln, our 16th president.

The Lincolns would eventually move away from Kentucky and settle in Indiana and then finally in Illinois. But Abraham Lincoln's early years were spent here in Kentucky. At a time when our

country was sorely divided, house against house
and brother against brother, Lincoln saw the
wisdom in both the unity of the nation, and the
abolition of slavery.

Because of him, slavery died a rightful death,
and yet we are still "One nation under God, indi-
visible, with liberty and justice for all." I think
Lincoln's early years in the frontier of Kentucky
helped instill in him the wisdom of some of those
early heroes. And the echoes of that wisdom still
inspire us today.

We desperately need that wisdom.

You can't read a newspaper or watch TV and
not be convinced that we are in the process of
immense change in America. This is even more
true in Appalachia. For so long we depended on
coal, but now that is changing. For so long the
people here lived in isolation, but now we realize
that we must take part in the challenges and
burdens of the rest of America.

The answer to our problems is not entirely
economic. Sometimes people say to me, "If only
we had more money here in Appalachia." Or, "If
only we had more political clout."

What we really need is wisdom. We need the
wisdom to decide what to do with what we have.
We need wisdom to decide how to keep the best
of the past and combine it with the best of the
present to build a new frontier.

In our CAP family, we are always seeking

wisdom. And nowhere is it more important than in our work with families. Poverty puts terrible strain on families. The constant worry about money is only the beginning. Maybe even more important is the despair and helplessness that poverty so often brings to both the old and young. These feelings make it difficult for family members to grow and adapt.

Like the heroes of wisdom from our past, I think we need to know when to preserve unity and when to stand apart. Our first goal is always to keep families together because we believe that strong families are Appalachia's biggest asset.

When we help children in our child development centers, for example, we also find out about the parents, and their needs and problems. Our goal is to help families persevere through hard times, and come through whole, so children can learn from the love and respect of their parents.

One of the problems in Appalachia is that too many children get married before they are truly ready. All it takes for two fourteen-year-olds to qualify for marriage is thirty dollars and parental consent. There's no wisdom in that. Most often, it is girls who suffer the most. They tend to be the younger member of the couple, and they soon discover they aren't really ready for the responsibilities of being a wife and mother. One of the things we try to do in our work with teenagers is convince them to wait. We try to show them that

they should finish their education before consider-
ing marriage.

Sometimes the problem of marrying too young,
combined with despair, leads to alcoholism and
child or spouse abuse. These families break my
heart. It's so hard to see what abuse can do to
women and children—and even sometimes men.
Even worse than the physical damage is the emotional wreckage caused by abuse.

That's why CAP has created three spouse abuse
shelters in the mountains to give women and
children a place of safety. Once the family is safe,
we help with reconciliation if that is what the
couple wants. We counsel husbands and wives to
help them heal wounds and learn to love again.
We try to regain the unity that is so important to
family life.

Sometimes unity is impossible. Abusive husbands are often unable to change, especially if they
refuse to accept that they have been abusive. When
that happens, we do everything we can to help the
wife and the children.

Brenda's husband Roy tried for years to find a decent job. He took part-time work whenever he could
find it, but it was never enough. Finally, after years
of trying, he just gave up. He became bitter and
angry, and began to drink heavily. When he drank,
he became violent towards both Brenda and her two
little girls. After five years of trying to cope with
this violence, Brenda was demoralized and shattered.

Finally, she escaped to Bethany House, one of

our spouse abuse shelters. While at Bethany
House, Tom, one of our counselors, talked to
Brenda about her goals and arranged for her to
take an aptitude test. When the test scores were
in, Tom asked Brenda if she had ever thought
about college. "College?" Brenda asked, "Are
you crazy? I'm 38 years old. I have two kids, no
car, no money, no place to live, and you want to
know if I've thought about college?"

Tom told Brenda about Family Life Services,
a CAP program that gives people a chance to start
over. Counselors like Tom help individuals and
families sort out their problems and find the
wisdom to make new choices. Then we help them
take those painful first steps toward a new life.

When Brenda got over her shock, she discovered
she really did want to attend college. We helped
her apply to Eastern Kentucky University where
she was eagerly accepted. Today, Brenda has a
college degree, two happy, well-adjusted children,
and a new husband.

To me, Bethany House and Family Life Services
are places where we teach wisdom. We help
people find the strength to make new choices and
change their lives for the better. I only wish we
could do more. I wish we could hire more
counselors to help couples sort out their problems,
and help abused women and children find peace
and hope.

I thank God we were able to help Brenda. When
she graduated from college last May, we all

cheered for her.

Brenda says, ''I can never repay all that has been given to me. And I can never give enough thanks to CAP's Bethany House and Family Life Services, and my counselor, Tom. But I owe my all to the Lord Jesus who allowed the most wonderful people in the world to come into my life.''

Brenda's words show great wisdom. I know when I feel most unsure about my life and the choices I must make, I find myself quietly going to church to visit my greatest hero of wisdom.

I remember that Jesus said, ''Seek ye first the things that are above. Seek ye first, the kingdom of God, and then all these other things will be given to you besides.'' He said, ''What does it profit you if you gain the whole world, and yet lose your very self.'' He told us to judge things as God judges them, not as men judge. These are the words of Jesus that continue to inspire me, and lead me to wisdom.

As I grow older, I find myself thinking of Solomon. When God offered Solomon one wish, he looked around at all the wealth and power that could be his, and told God he wanted only one thing: wisdom. I think that is my own wish. My greatest ambition is to gain a small measure of the wisdom of Solomon so I can be a better leader and help others find the wisdom to open this new frontier of the heart. Every night before I go to sleep, I say a simple prayer, ''Lord, lead thou me on. Show me the way. Give me wisdom.''

Heroes of Independence

I hate it when people say the road to independence is too hard. Sometimes, when I tell people my dream and my hope that the people of Appalachia can regain their independence, they tell me I'm out of my mind. "It'll never work," they say. That's when I tell them about one of my heroes, George Rogers Clark, and one of the most amazing stories I've ever heard.

The people who first crossed the mountains and settled in Appalachia had to be highly independent, cut off as they were from normal commerce and ruling authorities. So it's no surprise that when news slowly filtered through the mountains that something spectacular had happened in Philadelphia in July of 1776, it was met with great enthusiasm. Though the pioneers had their own concerns on the western edge of the frontier, they were eager to join in the battle for independence from Great Britain.

George Rogers Clark was one of the strongest independence backers. He worried that the British might attack and defeat the Kentucky settlements,

and therefore cut the colonies off from the West
and the Mississippi. He convinced Virginia leaders
to reassert their claim to Kentucky and give him
men and arms to defend the western frontier. That
seemed like a reasonable request. But Clark went
one step further. He also wanted to take the British
outposts at Kaskaskia and Vincennes in what is
now Illinois and Indiana, and the major British fort
at Detroit.

Clark got part of what he wanted. Virginia made
Kentucky a Virginia county, and therefore part of
the new United States of America. And they
authorized him to lead the defense of Kentucky.
Unfortunately, they gave him very few men to do
it with—and even less money.

But independence meant so much to George
Rogers Clark that he wasn't about to let a few set-
backs stand in the way of protecting that independence. With no real hope of success, he set
out with less than 200 men to cross hundreds of
miles of wilderness and defeat two British outposts
and a major fort.

Sometimes I feel as he must have felt. When
I want to help people get off welfare and stand
on their own two feet, I'm told that dependence
is too well ingrained. When I want to help Appalachia as a whole become less dependent on outside help and become a producer of prosperity,
I'm told that our economy is just too weak, and
our resources too scant.

And when I tell people what I hope CAP can do to help win independence for the people of Appalachia, they tell me, ''You can't possibly do that with so few people.''

Whenever I start to doubt what we can do, whenever I find myself believing the naysayers, I remember George Rogers Clark and the brave men who followed him.

Clark set out on his fateful trip in May of 1778. He and his men traveled several hundred miles down the Ohio River to the mouth of the Tennessee River and up through thick forests to Kaskaskia. There they caught the small fort off guard and captured it with barely a shot fired.

When the British heard of this audacity, they sent a force from Detroit to their remaining outpost at Vincennes on the Wabash River. Because it was the dead of winter, Clark correctly deduced that the British would wait until spring to attempt to retake Kaskaskia. Rather than wait for that, he and his men set out, on the fifth of February, to surprise and capture Vincennes for the United States of America.

The 150 miles from Kaskaskia to Vincennes led across an unbroken winter wilderness. It rained constantly and Clark's men had to fight off depression and despair as they slopped through mile after mile of mud and water. On the thirteenth of February, the small army came to the Little Wabash River. The constant rain had flooded the river, and ahead of Clark's band lay miles of land covered with nearly four feet of frigid water. It looked hopeless, and if they had given up at that point, history would not have faulted them. But the call of independence and freedom was too strong for those men to turn back.

They continued over the Little Wabash, over the Embarrass River, and through the nine miles of swollen swamp land between the Embarrass and the Wabash, where Vincennes lay unaware. The ordeal was so difficult that, although they felt a great need for haste, it took Clark's tiny army ten days to cover the roughly forty miles from the Little Wabash to Vincennes—only about four miles a day. By the end, many of these hardy frontiersman were so exhausted they could hardly stand.

I think of those men whenever I find myself believing those who say that independence is too big a goal, too hard to gain.

Because they valued freedom so much, Clark's men endured a trial that no other army has ever been through. After their incredible journey through Illinois, they captured Vincennes by surprise, and eventually pushed on to take Detroit. In doing so, this small band of less than 200 men—heroes of independence—secured the western border of the new United States, and played a major role in the birth of a great nation.

That's what a few good people can do when they

value independence and freedom. It's that strong a calling.

There is nothing in America that we treasure more highly than freedom. And I think we have seen that we are not alone in this very human desire. I believe the communist world has collapsed, not so much because of economics, but because the people wanted to be free. They wanted to chart their own course.

That's why the loss of independence in Appalachia makes me so sad. Too many people are on welfare. In many counties more than 40% of people live below the federal poverty line. Welfare and food stamps help keep people alive, but there is a serious loss of independence that comes with those programs. The people feel they are dependent on, and controlled by, a big, distant government—exactly what George Rogers Clark and his army fought so valiantly against.

That's why I love to remind the people of Appalachia how hard their ancestors fought for independence. The flame of freedom still flickers in the hearts of these people, and if I can fan it, I know it can become a bonfire to light the way to a new frontier.

Independence and freedom are central to everything we do at CAP.

In many poor communities, we operate what we call "Attic stores." At these stores we sell clothing and household essentials donated by people and companies all over the country. It may seem at first uncharitable, but, except in the case of emergencies, we rarely give these items away. The last thing we want to do is give handouts because handouts just make people dependent. We don't want people to think the best they can do is beg, so we charge nominal prices for all our items. Sometimes it's just a quarter or a dime, but it's important to allow poverty-stricken families to retain their pride in independence.

I believe very strongly that we must help local communities help themselves. Last year, I was proud that we helped three local women set up an Attic store in a poverty-stricken Appalachian community.

The store, which they call the Bread of Life Attic, grew out of the work these three wonderful women were already doing out of their own homes to help their neighbors. CAP helped them rent a small building and we supplied clothing and other items to expand their work. The Bread of Life Attic also operates a food pantry where poor families can get low priced food. They've helped dozens of local families cope with burnouts and other tragedies.

Now we are assisting them in expanding into an old unused grocery store. With the freezers and other grocery store fixtures, they'll be able to greatly expand their food pantry efforts.

This is a wonderful example of how a simple

helping hand can build independence instead of dependence. Not only is the Bread of Life Attic helping local families remain independent, but because it was formed and is operated by local people, the community as a whole has grown more independent.

Often we are asked to help families who are in emergency need of money. Their electricity may have been shut off, or the rent is overdue, or the cupboard is bare. We could simply turn our backs, or we could simply hand them a check. But there is another, better way. What we do is provide the help families desperately need, and then we give them the opportunity to pay us back by volunteering. Most jump at the chance. By doing this, we gain an enormous amount of volunteer labor for our other programs, as well as the creativity and insights of the mountain people. The people who volunteer, many of whom have been out of work for years, keep their independence, and also get a chance to experience the joy that comes from doing good work.

We in the CAP family, like George Rogers Clark, are still trying to set our people free. Step by step, we wade through the floods and the swamps. We explore the uncharted wilderness, willing to pay the price to set our people free.

When I think of George Rogers Clark and his army, I am reminded of my greatest hero of independence—another man who endured great suffering to win freedom for many.

Jesus told us, "If you remain in My word, you will truly be My disciples, and you will know the truth, and the truth will set you free."

But Jesus knew, like George Rogers Clark and the other leaders of our Revolution, that words alone can not win freedom. That famous Declaration in Philadelphia had to be backed up by men and women willing to lay down their lives.

I think that's why Jesus allowed Himself to be led to Pilate and to be put on the cross. Imagine what He went through. One of His closest friends betrayed Him for 30 pieces of silver. In His darkest hour of need, all His friends abandoned Him. That pain, and the pain of knowing what was about to happen to Him was so great that even He, who had been so sure of His mission, broke down and asked God to change the plan.

Then He was tortured, interrogated, and ridiculed by the high priests, and Pilate. In the end, they said He was a blasphemer, a man who hated God—a blow that must have hurt Jesus very badly. On His terrible journey through the streets of Jerusalem, He heard all those whom He had helped crying, "Crucify Him! Crucify Him!" After all of that enormous emotional pain, He was subjected to the physical agony of crucifixion, which was considered the most terrible way to die.

I wonder, why did He endure all that? It wasn't because He was guilty. Or because He had failed.

He endured it all to set us free, you and me, so that we may have the courage of free men and women.

Jesus said His death would be to ensure that all had a place in heaven; that all men and women would be equal and free.

So whenever I see people who live with too little freedom and independence in Appalachia, I think of heroes of independence like Jesus and George Rogers Clark. And I remind myself that freedom and independence are often very costly to win. But a new frontier of the heart can only be created where freedom sings, and independence is the right of every man, woman, and child.

Isolation and loneliness are common problems in
Appalachia — especially for the elderly.

Photo by Joe Foley

CAP volunteers and employees work with all age groups: children, teens, adults, and the elderly.

Photo by Judi Jackson

Photo: CAP Archives

Substandard housing is a problem in Appalachia.
Burnouts (top) are a problem, especially in the winter
months. CAP's Home Repair program strives to make
homes safe and warm.

Photo by Jeff Rogers

The young man in the apron is learning food preparation at CAPRICE (Christian Appalachian Project Resources for Independence and Community Employment) – a CAP program that helps people with disabilities work toward independence and self-sufficiency.

If the cycle of poverty in Appalachia is ever to end, more adult education programs are needed.

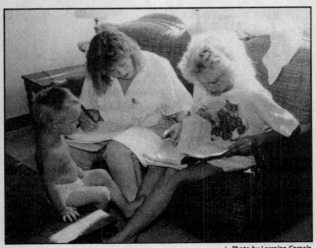

Photo: CAP Archives

CAP's Child Development Centers enable children in Appalachia to get a good start in their education — which is critically important to their future.

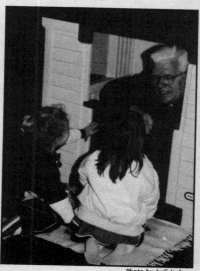

Photo by Judi Jackson

With more than 2,000 Christmas baskets to distribute
to poor families in Appalachia, CAP workers have to
start preparing months in advance.

It takes healthy minds and bodies to succeed in life. At CAP's summer camps, Appalachian children have an opportunity to meet new friends, to experience new activities, and be challenged to dream.

Heroes of Friendship

These days, we think of a neighbor as a good thing to have. But in the early pioneer days, neighborliness was more than that—it was a matter of survival. Isolated from normal channels of commerce and security, the pioneers had to rely on each other. They helped each other build houses and forts. They helped each other clear fields and plant crops. They protected each other from danger.

The isolation of the frontier made loneliness a serious problem. The pioneers gave each other companionship and entertainment. They prayed and mourned and shared their joys together.

Neighbors didn't need to be right next door. Often there were miles between homes, but still the power of friendship helped all survive. Sometimes the friendship of a neighbor would come from even farther away. One of my heroes of friendship is Dr. George Hart. He was a successful physician in Pennsylvania, but when he heard that the struggling settlement of Harrodsburg needed a doctor, he picked up his stakes and set off down the Ohio River. After a long, dangerous journey, he reached the tiny settlement and offered his service as a neighbor. In doing so, Dr. Hart became the first doctor in Kentucky, and in my mind, a hero.

In a similar story, Mrs. Jane Coomes, a woman trained as a school teacher, also found her way to Harrodsburg and offered to start the first school. The pioneer parents were thrilled to have the help of such a neighbor, and they all pitched in to build a small log-cabin schoolhouse. Jane Coomes became the first school teacher in Kentucky, and another one of my heroes of friendship.

There were easier ways for these two professionals to earn their living. There was a lot more security and opportunity in Pennsylvania, and the settlers in Harrodsburg couldn't pay much. But Dr. Hart and Mrs. Coomes saw the need of their distant neighbors and came to their aid.

Because of neighbors like these, the settlements of Appalachia grew rapidly, and those heroes of friendship left a legacy that continues in the mountains. One of the most beautiful traits of their descendants in Appalachia is the ability and the desire to be friends.

I was reminded of this powerful force recently when I met Jason and his wife, Helen.

Jason is an old man, worn down by the ravages of black lung disease from a lifetime of work in the coal mines. Jason and Helen live in a very

simple old house perched on the side of a mountain they call "Happy Top."

I had never met this couple before, yet they
made me feel like a long-lost kinsman. They gave
me the seat of honor in their small living room.
The old chair wasn't one that would mean much
to most people, but I felt like a king. They offered
me something to eat and drink, and we had a very
pleasant conversation.

Then Jason pulled me aside and asked if I'd like
to see something special. He led me outside and
we climbed a small bank. When we reached the
end of the trail, there was a one-room mountain
shed on a little bench of land sticking out from
the side of the mountain. We sat on the porch in
two rocking chairs and looked out over one of the
most remarkable views I have ever seen in all my
years in these mountains. Jason told me that he
and Helen often sat on that porch to find peace.
And sitting there with him I found that precious
commodity myself.

Jason's sharing of that special place with me was
one of the most moving demonstrations of friendship I have ever experienced.

The interesting thing about being a neighbor and
sharing friendship is that it doesn't have to be
expensive. Sometimes, the most valuable kinds of
friendship are the ones that cost the least—the
sharings of the heart.

This spirit of friendship still lives in Appalachia

today, but I am afraid that fewer and fewer heroes of friendship like Dr. Hart and Mrs. Coomes see our need from the outside and offer the outside aid of a friend. We have a real need for friendship here. Many of the young people have moved away to areas with more economic opportunity — leaving the elderly alone and isolated in the mountains. We need friends who can visit with the older folks and remind them that someone cares. And we need friends to show the young people how to build a new life here, instead of simply moving away.

Bringing in neighbors and friends from outside is critical to the work of the Christian Appalachian Project. In the last ten years, over 10,000 people have volunteered here in the mountains. Some were young people, fresh out of high school or college. Some were older, between careers, or even retired. Some stayed and put down roots when their volunteering was over. Others stayed for a few weeks or months and then went home again, having left their personal mark on Appalachia — and Appalachia on them.

When I talk to new volunteers, I always remind them that we are not here to judge or change people, but to offer the friendly hand of a neighbor, and show people new possibilities and opportunities. I was reminded how much this attitude means the other day when Linda, one of our volunteers, told me about Martha.

Martha is 26 years old. She and her husband and three children live in an old trailer deep in the back woods. Linda tutors Martha through our Adult Education Program. At Martha's kitchen table, they work together to help Martha gain her high school equivalency diploma.

Shortly after Linda began working with Martha, she got a call from a woman at a social service agency. The caller asked, "How often do you have to go to Martha's house?" Linda said she visited Martha once a week for an hour at a time. The caller was disgusted. "How can you stand being in that trailer for that long?" she asked.

Linda was insulted and felt the need to stick up for Martha. "It's not that bad," she said, "Martha does the best she can."

That week, when Linda drove up to Martha's house for their weekly lesson, she felt odd. For the first time, she really noticed the rust and rot on the trailer. She noticed how it leaned to one side and that half the windows were cracked. She felt the crunch of soda cans under the wheels of her car. The heap of trash in the middle of the yard looked like a mountain. She worried about the broken steps on the porch. When she knocked on the door, she realized she could see right into the house through cracks in the aluminum. Though Martha met Linda at the door with her usual bright smile, all Linda could see was the dirt inside the house. She noticed the ground beneath the trailer where it showed through the holes in the floor.

When Linda's eyes met Martha's, they both knew something was different.

But Linda suddenly realized that what she was seeing wasn't Martha, but Martha's surroundings. When she blinked and looked again, she saw Martha's hopeful smile, and her fierce determination to change her life. Though most people would be moved to despair by such a life, Martha has not given up. She dreams of becoming a nurse, and her courage to reach for this goal outshines all the dirt and erases all the other signs of poverty from her little house.

That day, Linda built Martha's reading lesson around a pamphlet entitled, "Helpful Hints to Keep a Clean House." Martha enjoyed it, and who knows, she may find a way to keep that old trailer clean in the future. But the important thing is that it will be her choice shared with her by a friend, and not a judgment imposed by an authority from outside.

Even if she doesn't become a better housekeeper overnight, Linda still feels that Martha is one of the most inspiring people she has ever met. Linda says Martha's courage to cope with the hand life has dealt to her—and to work for a better one— has helped Linda develop her own ability to persevere.

This is one of the most remarkable things about friendship and sharing as neighbors. So often, the one who gives gets even more in return.

The other day I received a letter from a wonderful lady who is 91 years old. She lives in Lincoln County, and our volunteers have been visiting her for some years. Her letter is so warm and grateful that I want to share it.

Dear Reverend Beiting,

I'm just a little old country lady. I have to use a walker to get around, as I am now 91 years old. My husband and I always wanted to have children but couldn't, and now that he's gone, your volunteers are my only family. I call them my children. I hope you will continue to share them with me.

All week long I look forward to Sunday afternoon when "my children" come to visit me. I am so grateful for them. I would love to meet you in person and give you a big hug to thank you.

I'd love to meet you sometime, but if we can't meet here in this life, we'll meet in God's heaven.

Your friend,
Betty

After reading such a letter, how can one have anything but the deepest admiration for volunteers who reach out with neighborly hands and say I love you? Like the old heroes of friendship, they give of themselves with no tangible benefit or reward.

On Valentine's Day I had the pleasure of meeting Betty in her home. She gave me that big hug she promised. She also had a red rose for me. Betty has had a serious stroke that makes it hard to understand her speech, but I had no trouble understanding her gratitude and love. I told her I wanted to put her letter in this book. She said, "Oh no! I'm not worthy of that."

Obviously, I disagree. Betty is a wonderful friend who gives back to our volunteers as least as much love as they give her.

I think the most beautiful of all the wonderful parables our Lord Jesus told us is one that describes friendship.

Jesus was asked by one of the scholars of the law about the commandment to "Love God, with all your heart, and love your neighbor as yourself." The Pharisee asked Jesus, "Who is my neighbor?" In answer, Jesus told him the parable of the Samaritan. He told him how a man was assaulted by robbers and left for dead. A priest and a Levite, both respected religious leaders, passed by without stopping. Finally, a Samaritan, a man shunned by polite society, came upon the robber's victim and was moved to help. He cared for the man and took him to an inn. He told the innkeeper he would pay any bills the robbers' victim ran up while he was recuperating.

When he finished the story, Jesus asked, "Which of these three was neighbor to the robbers' victim?'' The Pharisee answered, "The one who treated him with mercy."

Then Jesus gave one of the most simple, and beautiful directions of His entire ministry. He said, "Go and do likewise."

Jesus reminded us again and again that neighborliness is Godliness. At the Last Supper, He went beyond the commandment to "Love your neighbor as yourself." He told His Apostles He had a new commandment that went even further: "Love your neighbor as I have loved you."

When He told the disciples about the final judgment in heaven, He said the Lord would say, "Come you who are blessed by my Father. Inherit the kingdom prepared for you from the foundation of the world. For I was hungry and you gave me food, I was thirsty and you gave me drink, a stranger and you welcomed me, naked and you clothed me, ill and you cared for me, in prison and you visited me." Jesus said the righteous would ask the Lord, "When did we do these things?" and the Lord would answer, "Amen, I say to you, whatever you did for one of these least brothers of mine, you did for me."

It is in this spirit that our present day volunteers win my admiration as heroes of friendship.

In many ways, this kind of hero is the easiest to be. We often find it hard to imagine ourselves as courageous, or wise. But every one of us has the ability to be a hero or heroine of friendship. And with that power, we can change the world.

Heroes of Ingenuity

Whenever I come against an obstacle in my life and I run out of ideas, I think of the pioneers and say to myself, "What would I do if I were alone in the wilderness?"

Imagine what life was like then. There were no road maps. If you wanted to go somewhere, you had to find your own way. If you got lost, you couldn't ask directions at the local gas station. You found your way—or you died.

The pioneer women had to use a great deal of ingenuity every day of their lives. There were no conveniences. Every household task, from getting water to weaving cloth and making soap, was a challenge that took creative thinking to overcome. They had to figure out how to use and preserve new foods because otherwise, a crop failure could mean starvation. Ingenuity was a life and death thing back then.

One of my favorite stories about pioneer ingenuity concerns Simon Kenton. Kenton, like Daniel Boone, was a remarkable frontiersman. His exploits, including the fact that he saved Boone's life on more than one occasion, were known far and wide.

In June of 1780, however, Simon Kenton felt he was up against an impossible obstacle. The Revolutionary War was still raging, and a British and Indian force led by Captain Henry Byrd was assembled to capture the Kentucky territory and cut the new United States off from behind. Byrd's force included a large, wheeled brass cannon that tipped the balance of power in Kentucky sharply in favor of the British.

Byrd's men first used the cannon in an attack on Ruddel's Station. The stockade walls of the small settlement of Ruddel's Station had withstood many previous battles, but they had never faced artillery before. The very first cannonball collapsed the front wall of the fort. Without the protection of the stockade walls, the one hundred men and several hundred women and children of Ruddel's Station were easily defeated and captured by Byrd's army of 1,200 men.

When word of the cannon spread to Martin's Station, the next settlement in Byrd's path, the effect was paralyzing. Martin's Station surrendered without a shot being fired.

Frontiersman and adventurer Simon Kenton soon heard about the success of Byrd's army. He walked through the remains of Ruddel's Station, and learned of the surrender of Martin's Station. He was determined to do something to keep Byrd from winning the whole of Kentucky.

Kenton and a friend named Charles Gatliffe trailed Byrd's army to gain intelligence that might be useful to the defense of Kentucky. What really burned in Simon's heart, however, was to find a way to destroy that dreaded cannon. It seemed impossible that two men could possibly destroy a cannon protected by 1,200 men.

The pioneer spirit was not easily thwarted, however. A frontal attack was suicide, but if a thing couldn't be accomplished one way, it was time to find another. I often think that what we call "good old American ingenuity" was forged from the countless times pioneers had to make do, and find another way.

Kenton and Gatliffe watched from a safe distance as Byrd's army attempted to cross the Ohio River. All day long, men and supplies were ferried across by canoe. Suddenly, Kenton had a spark of inspiration. He and Gatliffe snuck close and hid in the brush on a spit of land that jutted into the river near where the canoes were crossing. For hours they lay perfectly still to avoid discovery. Finally, as night came, they saw their chance.

Five canoes pulled away from shore, and the last of Byrd's army began the crossing. Four of the canoes moved rapidly ahead, leaving one low-lying, slow-moving canoe in the rear. Though visibility was poor, Kenton knew the reason for the last canoe's sluggish progress.

It held the terrible cannon.

Hidden by darkness, Kenton and Gatliffe slipped into the water and swam to the canoe undetected. They tipped the canoe and sunk Byrd's brass cannon to the bottom of the Ohio River, where it probably still sits today.

With Byrd's cannon gone, the pioneers again found the courage to defend their hard won settlements, and the British campaign to capture Kentucky failed, largely as a result of the ingenuity of just two men.

I love this story because I think it shows what can be done if we just put ingenuity to work. I often think of those old pioneers as heroes of ingenuity. It was their every breath.

Many of our problems these days, both in Appalachia and the rest of the country, seem so difficult because ingenuity has become a lost art.

It's not easy to keep ingenuity alive in Appalachia today. For so long, the answer was always coal. If a town needed industry, the answer was coal. If an area was economically depressed, the answer was coal.

When the coal industry started to decline, a new ingenuity killer stepped in — dependency. Nowadays, we have become so dependent on government help that communities no longer even try to solve their own problems. Got a problem? Call a Representative. Still can't fix it? Call a Senator.

We look to the government as the source of solutions.

Solutions come from people who have to cope with problems. That's why CAP has always resisted the idea of solving people's problems for them. I want to give them the means and the inspiration to solve their own problems.

When my life is over, I hope what people remember about me is not "Reverend Beiting, he solved my problems for me," but "Reverend Beiting, he helped me find my own way out."

If that has been my legacy, then it will endure. Everything else we can do for the people of Appalachia is temporary. The one lasting change we can make is to teach people to think for themselves again. Think of new ideas. Think of new dreams. Plan a new future.

This was reinforced the other day in my own back yard where I have a lovely flower garden. The other day, as I was weeding the garden, two young brothers who live in the neighborhood came to me and said, "Can we help you, Reverend? We can pull up those things, too."

I must be getting cranky in my old age because I have to admit, my first thought was "No. Go away. I'll take care of this." My second thought was "Okay, you can help, but only if you sit right in front of me so I can tell you exactly which weeds to pull, and which flowers to leave."

Luckily, I went with my third thought which was

"Sure, let me show you how to do it." Then I showed the boys which ones were weeds and which ones were flowers. I told them "Pull the weeds and don't hurt the flowers."

With tremendous enthusiasm, the two little boys began to help me weed. Before long they had a nice pile of weeds . . . as well as pansies, marigolds, and petunias. It seemed that half my beautiful garden was in that pile.

I went back to the beginning and showed the boys again how to tell the weeds from the flowers. This time at least one of them caught on. A few minutes later I overheard him say to his brother, "Kevin, that's not a weed. That's a flower. Don't you dare pull that out."

This story says something important about how we can rebuild Appalachia. There is no doubt I could have weeded the garden faster by myself— and saved a great number of flowers. But then the kids wouldn't have learned anything and I would have just squashed their youthful enthusiasm.

I could also have stood over their shoulders every minute saying, "Pick that one. Don't pick that one. Pick that one. Don't pick that one." If I had done that, again, the boys wouldn't have learned anything.

Instead, I took a chance. I gave the boys the information they needed, and then I let them work out their own solutions. In the end, they found a sense of satisfaction they would never have gotten if I'd turned them away or guided their every move. The next time they need to weed a garden they'll know where to start.

We could just turn our backs on the brutal poverty in these mountains and it would probably continue indefinitely. Or we could try to solve the problems with money. The federal government tried that in the 60s with the "War on Poverty." It did a lot of good, but poverty is still with us because the people didn't learn to permanently erase it on their own.

They didn't revive the lost art of ingenuity.

When I gather with people to embark on some goal, I usually say "Let's just sit here for a few moments. Let's think what we're going to do. Let's use a little ingenuity." Sometimes they tell me, "Oh let's just get started. Let's get busy."

I say we're not just supposed to be busy. We're supposed to be thinkers and planners. When I put it that way, people get excited. There's a wonderful satisfaction that comes from being creative and using ingenuity.

Letting people use their ingenuity makes them creators like the Almighty in heaven instead of machines carrying out someone else's wishes. That's a powerful difference and I believe it's the way God wants us to work.

Just a little over a year or so ago, we formed a new corporation called the Appalachian Development Corporation. Its function is to find new solutions. We are working with community and government leaders to bring new industries to this area. It's not an easy job. We have a lot of disadvantages. Even finding good building sites in this mountainous area can be a problem. But we have a lot of advantages as well. We have people who really need to work. The mountain people have survived with adversity for so long that they have a great desire to overcome.

What we need is ingenuity to find ways to overcome our disadvantages and make the best use of our many advantages.

One of my favorite examples of how we have imitated the pioneer heroes of ingenuity is a program we call Operation Sharing.

Over the years, we have occasionally received donations of merchandise that corporations and individuals no longer needed. Sometimes it was overstocked or out of date merchandise. Other times it was used, but still useful. We've received everything from a truckload of toothbrushes to a prime breeding bull. A few years ago, we decided to turn this effort into a real force for change in Appalachia. We began to actively solicit surplus materials and the response has been amazing. Last year we received more than $19 million dollars in donated merchandise.

But that's only the beginning. Once we have the supplies, we have to figure out how best to use them to help the people of Appalachia. We distributed the toothbrushes, for example, to our own public health programs and health and dental agencies all over Appalachia. Hygiene and health are two major problems that often accompany poverty. Many of the children who received toothbrushes had never seen one before.

Many of those same children live in what can barely be called shacks. The state of housing in Appalachia is often appalling. I can't tell you how many times I've stood in kitchens with holes in the floor and watched water pour through the roof, and felt the cold wind whistle through cracks in the wall. Many people don't have running water and still use outhouses.

That's why we especially appreciate donations of building materials, which we put to very good use in our home repair program. In this program we provide materials, expertise, and volunteer labor to help people rebuild their homes. Not only does this improve their lives directly, but it gives them a new pride in themselves and their lives.

There is a woman named Ruth who glows with that new pride. Ruth lives far off the main road in Jackson County, Kentucky. She is 76 years old and ever since her husband died some years ago, she has watched with dismay as her old house crumbled around her. As the house deteriorated, it became drafty and cold. Ruth practically lived her whole life within a few feet of her large wood stove. Even so, she was always bundled up, wearing a heavy sweater and her best boots. The wind howled right through the old walls, and even with the wood stove, Ruth was always cold.

When Ruth's plight came to our attention, we sent one of our home repair crews to inspect her home. In addition to the bad walls, the crew also recognized that Ruth's porch was dangerously weak. As soon as we could, we sent the crew back out with building supplies. Aided by a team of college students who had volunteered with our home repair program, we replaced the damaged siding and rebuilt Ruth's porch. We even added a railing to make the porch safer for her.

If you go to Ruth's house today, you may find that, out of habit, she still huddles around her wood stove. With pride in her voice, however, Ruth will tell that the house is much warmer and drier. If you have time, she'll give you the grand tour of her new porch.

Sometimes the benefits of Operation Sharing are important in emotional ways. One of our great friends, a New Jersey woman named Carole Johnson, has created a network of volunteer seamstresses across the country. She and her helpers sew little girl's dresses and donate them to Operation Sharing. Last year, when we brought five tons of Operation Sharing supplies to the town of Sneedville, Tennessee, everyone was glad for the furniture and the dental supplies and the toys, but the big excitement was Carole's dresses.

Sneedville has had more than its share of hard luck in recent years. The big zinc mine's vein ran out and closed more than a decade ago. Since then, no other industry has replaced this major employer. Far from a major highway or airport, Sneedville has been forgotten, and the scarcity of good jobs has plunged many families into poverty.

Imagine what those dresses mean to the little girls of Sneedville, many of whom have never had any nice clothes before. Each dress is different, and each one is beautiful. They made a lot of little girls feel unique and worthwhile. That's a wonderful thing.

These are just a few ways that we try to take the generosity of our supporters and our Operation Sharing donors and turn it into something beautiful.

I am convinced that this creative ingenuity is God's plan for Appalachia—and the rest of the world as well.

Jesus told the Apostles that God answers our prayers—but He didn't say how. When we think we haven't gotten an answer, it's because we haven't used our God-given ingenuity. God gives us what we need, but sometimes we don't recognize it because we've lost the art of ingenuity.

For a long time, Appalachia has faced what seem like insurmountable obstacles of poverty. We can accept this fate, or we can lie down and die, but I don't think that's right. I know it's not what God

wants for his people in Appalachia. I know if we
keep the pioneer heroes of ingenuity in our hearts
and if we use the wisdom and creativity God gave
us, we can overcome all the seemingly insurmountable obstacles and build a new frontier.

Heroes of Determination

There is one thing the people of Appalachia have never lost. Some have forgotten how to dream, others have lost the pioneer love of freedom, and many have lost hope. But the one thing I admire most about the people of the mountains is that they have the most remarkable determination to survive and prevail. This trait carries right back to the pioneer days.

To settle a new land, the early heroes of Appalachia must have had incredible determination—determination to survive, determination to endure, determination to build a new home and a new world. Of all of those old heroes of determination, I think the most remarkable is Jenny Wiley.

Jenny Wiley was one of those incredibly brave pioneer women who ventured with their families into the unknown land over the mountains. When men like Daniel Boone set out alone into the wilderness, it obviously took a lot of courage. But it has always struck me that it took an even greater level of courage to bring a family into the wilderness. Jenny Wiley had that kind of courage.

Even more so than Jenny Wiley's courage, I'm inspired by the incredible determination she showed in the most difficult episode of her life. On an October day in 1789, a group of Cherokee and Shawnee descended on Jenny Wiley's small cabin near Walker's Creek. They mistook her home for that of a man who had ruthlessly hunted and killed their people for years. Bent on revenge, they killed Jenny Wiley's children and her teenage brother before they realized their error.

Jenny Wiley was just weeks from giving birth to another child, but she was taken captive and held for months, during which time the child was born and killed. All of this incredible tragedy, born out of the senseless cycle of violence and revenge that characterized so much of the early relations between the settlers and the Native Americans, would have broken the heart of the average person.

Jenny Wiley refused to give up. As the weeks slipped by, she watched for a chance to escape. She was tied to the stake and threatened with burning, but her composure and her refusal to break so impressed the Cherokee and Shawnee that they relented and let her live. One day, when the band went hunting, they left Jenny Wiley tied to a tree with deerskin thongs. It began to rain as she stood helplessly tied to the tree. I can imagine the raindrops mixing with poor Jenny Wiley's tears of despair. Still she didn't quit.

She noticed she could move her arms a bit. The rain was making the deerskin stretch. Little by little, Jenny Wiley wriggled and pulled—and finally she was free!

She ran off into the woods and eluded her captors in their attempts to retake her. For several days she waded through icy brooks and forged her way through dense forests. On and on she struggled. Finally, she found her way to the Louisa River near her home. She saw a neighbor loading a log raft on the other side of the river. Jenny called to him and the friend rushed over and brought her safely back to the other side just as the Cherokee and Shawnee arrived at the spot where Jenny had stood moments before. A short while later Jenny Wiley arrived safely home into the arms of her overjoyed husband, and took her place in the folklore of Appalachia.

Not far from where I live is a Kentucky State Park named after Jenny Wiley. Whenever I visit this lovely spot, I think of Jenny Wiley and her incredible story of determination. She is my hero when the days seem darkest. When I'm feeling so old and worn that I can't go on anymore, I remember her. When I'm discouraged by the results of my work, I recall her determination. Those are the times when Jenny Wiley means the most to me.

This woman faced hardships far greater than any

I have ever faced. Having lost five young children and a brother, she lived with a broken heart that I can scarcely imagine.

Still she never gave up. Never.

Because of her determination, she lived to the age of seventy-one, a ripe old age for a pioneer woman.

Jenny Wiley was not the only one who had this kind of determination in the early days of Appalachia. Fierce determination was a trait most of the pioneers shared. I think that kind of determination lives on in the people of Appalachia today.

Often they live under conditions that people in other parts of the country wouldn't be able to stand. Many don't have indoor plumbing, some have no electricity. I have met many older men and women in their seventies, and even eighties, who still chop their own firewood, and carry water from distant wells.

The people of the mountains have to cope with incredible poverty and isolation, but they never quit. Because so many homes are heated with old coal stoves, and run with ancient electrical wiring, fires are very common. When the nearest fire truck is fifteen to twenty five miles away on back country roads, the usual result is a house burned to the ground. Still, like Jenny Wiley, they don't quit.

Our emergency assistance program, with the help of CAP's friends, reaches out to families facing great hardship and supports them in their determination. Sometimes it isn't so much what we do, but that families know someone cares about them and understands their struggle.

Three years ago, Paul and Marlene lost their home and all their belongings to a fire. They moved their two small children into a rented trailer. Paul was doing everything he could to support his little family, but the best job he could find was part-time at a fast food restaurant at $4.40 per hour. Six months later, they had fallen behind on their rent and their landlord was threatening to evict them. On top of this they had large overdue medical bills.

When we heard about their plight, we did what we could. I only wish it could have been more. We were able to help them pay their rent and we provided some clothes for the children. It didn't seem like much, but our concern, coupled with Paul and Marlene's own powerful determination, made a big difference.

Paul says our assistance helped convince him to keep trying. Like Jenny Wiley, this family never quit, and it's paid off. Today both Paul and Marlene are working and they have been able to catch up on their bills and have even worked out a deal with their landlord to purchase the trailer they have been renting. It's no palace, to be sure, but it's their home now.

Their story shows how a simple helping hand

can provide hope to support a family's determination to prevail.

Sometimes, however, despair overwhelms determination—that's what happened to John, a man I met recently. When I walked across a swinging bridge over a creek to get to John's house, it wasn't hard to see why he might despair. The house he lived in with his wife and five children was falling apart. John had asked me to visit him because his electric stove had caught fire because of bad wiring. John was just barely able to put the fire out before it destroyed the whole house. He hoped I could help him rewire his house to make it safe.

As John took me through the house, I saw that a burned stove and bad wiring were the least of his problems. The uninsulated house was cold and drafty. The roof leaked, the walls sagged, and the floors were rotting.

I told John, "There is no sensible way you can repair this house. You'd be throwing good money after bad, and you still won't have a decent place for your family to live."

With despair clouding his eyes John said, "What am I supposed to do? I don't have the money for a new house, and I have no way to get it."

"How do you know that," I said, "What if we could get some lumber? Do you have any relatives or friends who would help you build?"

He thought for a long minute, and I could almost

see the cloud of despair melt away, and that old pioneer determination begin to shine through. "Well," he said finally, "You know, my brother would help, and I think my cousin, and there's a neighbor down the road who owes me a favor. He'd probably chip in."

Almost before I knew it, John was excited, and determined to make something new and better for his family. We've promised to provide him with some lumber, and help to get a place cleared for a small house, and he's applying for a loan. Suddenly, he has a whole new vision and a stubborn determination to see it happen.

Now that we've created a dream and awakened his natural determination, I have no doubt that John will succeed. Soon there will be one less family living in a dangerous, cold shack in Appalachia. That's what the example of Jenny Wiley can do.

Jenny Wiley is not my only hero of determination. I also think of my own father.

My father was born in 1901. He witnessed the disasters of World War I even though he was not yet old enough to fight. He was married during the roaring '20s and then watched as the world crashed in the Great Depression.

He endured when his training as a carpenter became all but useless when the Depression brought construction to a halt. He had to swallow a great deal of pride to take a job with the Works Progress Administration (WPA), a government

work program for the poor. That work wasn't
enough to support a growing family, so he sold
household cleaning products door-to-door in the
evenings. On Saturdays, he did whatever odd
carpentry jobs he could find.

Like so many people in those days, he never
gave up. He was determined to make it — that all
of us would make it. He had only a sixth grade
education, but treasured education deeply, and he
made sure every one of his eleven children
graduated from high school. He urged me to go
further, and I became the first member of our family in two generations to get a college degree.

My parents' determination had a great influence
on all their children and grandchildren and I'm
very proud of what this family has done. My
brothers and sisters and their children have helped
me enormously in my work in the mountains.
They've also done a great deal on their own to
help the poor and the elderly in their own
communities.

I think we've been able to do good things
because my father taught us never to quit. There
is always a tomorrow — always another chance as
long as you don't give up.

I believe in that idea. It's what made it possible
for a few determined people to change the course
of America's history.

One of the things that sustained the pioneers in
their determination was their faith in God. As

inheritors of the great Judeo-Christian tradition we should never give up. The Bible says, "The Lord is my shepherd, of whom should I be afraid?" And "If God be for us, who can be against us?"

God tells us through His Word that He holds us in the palm of His hand, and that we are the apple of His eye. With such a powerful backer, we should never, ever despair. We should be heroes of determination.

This is one of the guiding principles of our work at CAP. Our mission has not been easy. When I was a young man, I thought I could erase poverty in the mountains in ten, maybe fifteen years at most. Now I realize that the prize does not necessarily go to the strongest, or the fastest, but to the one with the most determination. There is great truth in that simple childhood tale of the turtle and the hare.

We are determined to endure. We shall overcome. One day we'll see the night of despair disappear and the light of hope rise on a new frontier.

Heroes of Hope

The most beautiful word in the English language is "hope." This one word captures the feeling that our lives make a difference, and that the future will be better than the past.

We're all born with this wonder of hope, but it's an easy thing to lose. That's why I've always been inspired by heroes and heroines of hope, those who hold on when everyone else has given in to despair—the enemy of hope.

There were certainly heroes of hope among the early pioneers. Only the mystery of hope allowed them to brave the dangers they faced, and undertake the enormous task of building a new land under such difficult conditions.

One of my favorite heroes of hope is a woman I had the pleasure to meet before she passed away in 1965. Her name was Mary Breckinridge. Her work began in the 1920s, when the ancient battle between hope and despair had turned to despair's favor in Appalachia.

Mary Breckinridge faced more than her fair share of heartache. Her first husband died just two years after their marriage, a loss Mary mourned for the rest of her life. Six years later, she married again and when her first child, whom she always called "Breckie," was born two years after that, Mary was deliriously happy. Unfortunately, her happiness was short-lived. Two years later, Mary's second child—a baby girl—was born prematurely, and died before her first day was over. Less than two years after that, just after his fourth birthday, Mary's pride and joy, her little Breckie, became seriously ill and also died.

If Mary Breckinridge had lost all hope at that point in her life, it wouldn't have been surprising, but she didn't. She dedicated her life to improving the health and welfare of children. After gaining training and experience in caring for children and mothers in France during World War I, Mary came home to America and looked for a place to put her hope to the test.

By the 1920s, hard times had already befallen the mountains of Kentucky and many other Appalachian regions—and despair proudly walked the land. Modernization had passed by this region, leaving its people isolated and poor. No paved roads existed. The yearly income of families in the region was half that of the rest of the country. In many counties there were no doctors or nurses.

Mary looked this despair in the eye and saw the ultimate challenge of her hope. Because she knew that the health of children depended so much on

a healthy birth and a healthy mother, Mary felt
the best way to help children was to help their
mothers. Rather than throw out the midwife tradition that had served this area since the frontier
days, she tried to update that tradition with the
knowledge of modern medicine. The result was
the Frontier Nursing Service, the first major use
of nurse-midwives in this country's history. The
Frontier Nursing Service's midwives, ''angels on
horseback,'' as they were called, traveled the
countryside assisting at births, and administering
basic health care to families.

One of the reasons the Frontier Nursing Service was so successful for nearly fifty years was
that Mary always honored the dignity of the people
she tried to help, something we try very hard to
duplicate at CAP. She saw the poverty, and the
ill health, and she fought that with all her heart.
But she also saw the independence and courage
of the mountain people, and she loved that with
all her soul.

In her autobiography, Mary wrote quite mov-
ingly about a young orphan boy named Joe
Morgan. Joe lived with neighbors until he devel-
oped a serious heart condition. When Joe's health
worsened, he was brought to the Frontier Nursing Service's main clinic. The first thing he did
upon arrival was to thank Mary for a blanket she
had sent him. His heart condition caused poor cir-
culation, and little Joe was always cold. After

thanking Mary for that kindness, he asked if she could write a letter to the neighbors who had cared for him all those years. Then he pulled a nickel out of his pocket, all the money he had in the world, and said, "If you bust this nickel, you can pay for a stamp for that thar letter."

Several days later, young Joe Morgan died. Mary wrote in her book,

Of all the children I have known in the mountains, Joe has left the most unfading imprint on my memory. This homeless boy of eleven, whose mother had died in childbirth, whose father had been a moonshiner and was serving his time in Federal jail, this boy who thanked you for sending him a warm wrap to cover him, who thought of a thank you letter to his host and paid for the stamp himself out of the only nickel he had in the world, who bore uncomplainingly the pangs of his mortal illness and twelve hours of exhausting travel, this waif, with a knightly code of courtesy and honor—whenever I think of him I recall the divine promise: "And they shall be mine, saith the Lord of hosts, in that day when I make up my jewels."[2]

---

2. Wide Neighborhoods, Mary Breckinridge, The University Press of Kentucky, 1981.

Though Mary faced this kind of heartbreak again and again in her life, she never lost hope. When I met her, towards the end of her life, I could still see in her eyes the boundless hope that enabled her to mesmerize audiences when she traveled the country raising money for the Frontier Nursing Service.

Over the years, the Frontier Nursing Service helped deliver almost 15,000 babies, with only nine maternal deaths — a record far better than the rest of the country, with its hospitals and doctors. The Frontier Nursing Service provided more than a million vaccinations to children, and treated more than 57,000 patients for various illnesses.

Most importantly, the "angels on horseback" brought hope to the mountains. That's why Mary Breckinridge is one of my favorite heroes.

In our work at CAP we constantly battle despair. We face enormous problems. In some counties, one out of seven homes is without running water, and even more are without indoor bathrooms. In many counties, 40% of the children live in families with incomes under the federal poverty level. Only 50% of adults have a high school diploma.

In the face of these problems, we strive to carry on Mary Breckinridge's vision of hope for the children. We know, as she did, that often that means helping both parents and children.

Jane and her family present a wonderful example of how much of a difference this can make. Jane's little girl, Megan, was born with severe hearing loss. At the age of three, Megan couldn't talk. The poor little girl was so frustrated that when she needed something, she would yell loudly and hit to get attention. It was her only way to communicate. As a single mother facing terrible poverty in addition to this crisis, Jane was overwhelmed.

When Megan came to our child development center, where we try to help the children of poverty catch up before they enter first grade, we immediately recognized how bright she was. All she needed was help to communicate. We began to teach her sign language. Jane learned as well, and we showed her how to use a home-based sign language program to help Megan at home. Still, we knew it wasn't enough. We asked an expert from the Kentucky School for the Deaf to work with our child development center teachers to show them how to better help Megan.

Eventually, Jane and Megan's teachers came to the decision that Megan should attend the Kentucky School for the Deaf. We helped Jane arrange transportation to and from the school each day, so her little girl could continue to live at home.

While all this work was being done to help Megan, we had not forgotten Jane. We helped her brush up on her educational skills so she could apply to college and improve her ability to support her family.

Today, three years later, Megan is doing quite well, and has blossomed into a sweet, young girl. Jane is enrolled in Somerset Community College and dreaming of a bright future.

This is what hope does.

We could have looked at the desperate situation of this family and thrown up our hands in despair. But like my heroes of hope, we keep on trying. We know that with the help of our supporters, volunteers, and employees we make a difference.

Our Community Health Advocates Program (CHAP) is another way in which we follow Mary Breckinridge's example of hope. Though there are now a few hospitals and some doctors in this area, we are still plagued by bad health and limited health care services. When this leads to disease or disability, it only adds to poverty. CHAP helps bring public health information to families in isolated areas, and provides vital services to help them keep their precious health.

I think Mary Breckinridge would be proud that her dream of good health lives on.

A few years back, I bought a small trampoline to keep in my backyard. I'm too old to try the thing myself, but I bought it because my neighborhood is filled with young children. When they come to my house they always ask, "Can we jump?" I love to watch them soaring into the air, higher and higher each time. It often strikes me that hope is like a trampoline. Each time we let it win over despair, it takes us higher and higher.

When the children finish jumping, we sit down and say a prayer. We thank God for the green grass, and the sun, and the warmth of a spring day. We thank God for trampolines. We thank Him for hope that tomorrow will be a better day.

Many years ago, when I was preparing for the priesthood, we had to study the virtues of faith, hope, and charity. Hope was described as that sure confidence that great things can happen, if we are united with God, the source of all power. Hope is not based upon our strength alone, it is based on the confidence that there is a greater power we can add to our own.

One of the most interesting things I find in the Scriptures is that Jesus spoke far more about hope than even about love or faith. He told us to hope for greater things. He assured us that with Him we could do all things, that there was no reason to limit our dreams. He said, "Ask and you shall receive. Seek and you shall find. Knock and the door shall open."

That's why I can never give in to despair. Sometimes the problems in Appalachia seem overwhelming and I think, "Maybe I should stop. Maybe this is too hard." Then I remember that Jesus told me to follow Him, and I start to think, "Well, if I just do this thing, that will help. And maybe tomorrow will be better than today."

I think of that heroine of hope, Mary

Breckinridge. When her little Breckie lay dying, Mary leaned close to his face and heard his last words. "I twy to do wight," he told her in his little boy voice.

Just before his eyes closed for that last time, Mary whispered back, "I will try to do right, too."

That's all we have to do. We are not expected to change the world overnight. If we just keep hope alive and try to do right, it will turn out okay in the end.

As I share my dream of what is still to be in Appalachia with the people of my CAP family, I warn them, "Don't give in to despair. Let's keep hope alive, like the pioneers of old. With help from our friends around the country, we can make a difference. We can keep jumping a little higher on the trampoline of hope. Eventually, if we lighten our spirits with hope, we can soar on eagles' wings, and fly to a bright dawn over a new frontier of the heart.

Heroes of Faith

Jesus told us faith could move mountains. The pioneers of Appalachia didn't move the mountains, but they relied on faith to get them over the mountains. I have always been struck by the faith of those Appalachian pioneers. Their sense of protection from above gave them the courage to dream and to settle a new frontier.

In 1775, Benjamin Logan and a few companions started out with Daniel Boone and Colonel Henderson on the trail that would eventually lead to the settlement of Boonesborough. Before the group reached the eventual site of Boonesborough, however, Logan and his companions left the path to go their own way. It must have taken a lot of faith to do that. There was far greater security in the larger party.

Logan and his small band traveled further south and began to quickly build their own settlement. Within a short time, others came over the mountains to join them. One of those who came was a devout Welshman. When this man heard that Logan had first landed at the spot on May 1st, he suggested the settlement be named St. Asaph, because that day is the anniversary of the canonization of this sixth-century Welsh bishop. Logan, who was familiar with the beautiful psalms written by St. Asaph, thought this was a wonderful idea, and so St. Asaph became the name of the third settlement in Kentucky after Harrodsburg and Boonesborough.

As a Catholic priest, I'm proud that St. Asaph was named after a Catholic because I love my church. But even more, I'm proud that those early pioneers put such emphasis on faith.

When I reflect on my life and try to understand what has given me vitality, I think the answer is faith. It is my utter dependence on God that I find so exciting.

Today, at age 70, I look back to the first day I came to Appalachia, and what has happened since, and I am truly amazed. I could never have known in those early days what the future would be. If someone had told me what would take place, I would have thought them jesting.

If someone had told me my work would create an organization known as the Christian Appalachian Project that would, over the years, bring so much good to this region, I would have said, "That's too much to ask of one man." CAP now has 452 full and part-time employees, and close to 1,000 volunteers each year. It provides millions of dollars worth of emergency assistance, services, volunteer aid, and "in-kind" gifts like building supplies, clothes, and books to some of the most poverty-stricken counties in America.

If someone had told me CAP would gather numerous awards such as the "1993 Outstanding Philanthropic Organization Award" we received last year from the National Society of Fundraising Executives, I would have said "No way!"

I would've laughed and said, "No man could build that alone." I would've been absolutely right to laugh. Man alone has not wrought the miracle of the Christian Appalachian Project. Through every step of our development from a small second hand clothing store to one of the most respected and successful charities in the country, God's hand has guided our way.

If I have done anything right in all these years, it has been that I have lived my faith from morning till night.

From the very first, I held this great conviction tightly and it led to three principles for fighting poverty in Appalachia. First, I tried to find the root of the problem. I didn't act until I understood the cause, not just the symptom. Second, I tried to find solutions to the problem—solutions with a long-term view. Third, and most important, I always asked myself, "Why do you want to do this?"

If I wanted to create a project because I thought it would make me important, or make me well-known, I scrapped it right then and there. If I could honestly say, "This will help God's children, and bring God's love to the mountains," then I knew we were on to something important.

Once I reached that point there was no turning back. It never made any difference to me what hurdles had to be overcome. Jesus said faith could move mountains. How could I be worried about a lack of money or people to do God's work? If I was truly doing God's work, He would be beside me all the time, helping me find my way, convincing people to help with their donations of money and time. If I was right, and this was a project that God wanted done, nothing could ever stand in its way.

As I look back and see what we have accomplished, I am impressed by the magnitude of the changes we've made. I'm also painfully aware of what still remains. Too many people still live in leaking, staggering shacks that would, and should, be condemned as housing. I still, far too often, meet the despair created when entire families are without work and even worse, without hope of ever finding it. I still see far too many children who, because of the poverty and illiteracy of their parents, are so far behind before they even enter first grade, that no school system can hope to help them.

I still meet too many senior citizens who are so

isolated and lonely that they have nearly forgotten the joy of human companionship. And too many people still suffer the ill health that so often accompanies and feeds poverty.

I still hear far too few dreams.

But I can never despair. I know what we are doing is right. If I don't always see the end result, if the fruition comes after my own life is at an end, that is God's business. I firmly believe He has a plan to revive this part of the world, and we are simply following His outline.

We have to have faith.

Our Garden Seed program is a wonderful symbol of faith. Good nutrition is a major problem in Appalachia. Poverty often leads people to buy the cheapest possible food, which may not be the most nutritious. When you live with daily despair, it's hard to be overly concerned about your health. Through our Garden Seed program, so generously supported by our donors, we provide seeds and gardening help to thousands of families in Appalachia.

Can a few seeds change Appalachia? Maybe— and I recently saw a wonderful example of how.

Andrew and Sheila live in an old run-down house with their two boys, Matthew and Scott, and Andrew's mother, Mary. Out in back of their house is an even older one-room shack. A 90-year-old man named Authur has lived there longer than anyone can remember.

I suppose the condition of this family's poverty might cause some visitors to turn away, but if they did, they'd miss a wonderful sight. Out in back of the house is one of the most beautiful gardens anywhere. It is nearly two full acres, and planted with onions, beans, carrots, corn, cucumbers, cantaloupes, peas, and various flowers grown from CAP seeds.

Everyone in the family takes a hand in this garden, and it is a source of tremendous pride to all of them. All summer long they plant and harvest, and they freeze and can enough vegetables to last all winter. Even Authur, at his age, is out there every day all summer. He can neither read nor write, but Authur is a wonder in the garden.

What makes me most excited about this garden are the two rows off to the left. These belong to the boys. Last summer, ten-year-old Matthew planted onions, beans and carrots. Eight-year-old Scott planted corn, cucumbers, and cantaloupes. If you go to visit, they will proudly take you around and show you every plant and tell you how they care for it and how much they expect from it.

There is something wonderful happening here that goes far beyond a healthy diet. Those two boys are developing a sense of pride and accomplishment that can help them overcome the stigma and despair of poverty. Their house may never be on a Better Homes tour, but nobody has a more beautiful garden.

Giving seeds to families is a symbol of faith. When we put seeds in the ground, we have faith that, through God's miracles, crops will grow and develop into healthy food. My faith tells me that, through our Garden Seed program, we are planting the seeds of a rich harvest, especially for children like Matthew and Scott.

I feel the same way about our adult education classes. When we help a forty-year-old woman gain her high school equivalency diploma, we can't guarantee her she'll find a better job right away. Maybe all we are doing is opening doors for her down the road. Maybe all we are doing is equipping her to better help her children with their education so they will have a better chance than she had. The payoff might not be immediate, but faith tells me it will come.

When we repair a home and put in a bathroom and running water where there was none before, we improve the life of a family. But even more importantly, we help them find self-respect. This means far more than a toilet that flushes.

My faith tells me this is how we'll win the battle to open a new frontier of the heart.

Faith is contagious. When we have faith in God, it gives us faith in ourselves. When we have faith in ourselves, we have faith in others, and they gain faith in themselves. In this way, I hope we are building a solid chain of faith that will someday lock despair and poverty away from these beautiful hills.

Just the other day, I was speaking with a woman who is 72 years old. She recently retired from a long teaching career in California, and now she is thinking about becoming a volunteer. She asked me to pray for her to help her find the courage to make the difficult decision to leave her children and grandchildren in California and come here to the mountains to work. Instead, I told her to pray about it herself. Then I winked and said, "Because if you pray about it, God will push you into our camp."

It works both ways. The faith of the people who make up the CAP family constantly reinforces and strengthens my own faith. CAP is far more than just another charitable organization, or social agency. This is a wonderful family of men and women from all kinds of lives walking together in the Lord to do something remarkable. Each member brings his or her own skills, dreams, and type of religion, but they all work together as heroes of faith.

Beyond these people is a yet larger family of heroes—the thousands of people all across the country who send their gifts to help in this work. Most of those people will never get a chance to visit here and see how their generosity is making a difference, but they have the faith to do what they can to help.

The letters they write, the stories they tell, the enthusiasm they feel as they join us in this work is just wonderful. It's a revolution of a very powerful kind, and I feel proud to be a part of this sharing of God's love.

I think about my hero Daniel Boone. Towards the end of his life, a preacher approached him and asked him about his faith. He asked Daniel if he needed to learn about God. Daniel looked him in the eye and said, "No sir. I always loved God ever since I could recollect."

That's my goal for my life and for the Christian Appalachian Project. I hope that, like modern day heroes of Appalachia, we can open our hearts to create a new frontier.

My prayer is that when this journey is done, this enormous family of caring people all across the country will be a testimony to faith. I pray that through our deeds we can together say, "We always loved God ever since we could recollect."

Epilogue

When Dr. Thomas Walker passed through the narrow gap in the Appalachian Mountains that would come to be called the Cumberland Gap, he had no idea he was opening a new frontier. I am more purposely hopeful of my exploration.

I have enjoyed writing about my heroes. To me, they are more than just figures in history, they are friends. I walk with them and gain inspiration from them every day of my life. But I hope this book is more than just a description of some of my heroes. I hope that this book marks a new trail— one that leads to a new frontier of the heart.

At my age, life truly becomes a day to day proposition. I have no idea how many more years God will give to me.

I hope this book challenges you to think about being a hero in your own life. I hope it helps you find the courage to step into the unknown—to live with faith, to search for wisdom, to practice ingenuity, and to cultivate hope.

You are a special gift from God. He never has, and never will, make another one like you. You were made to be a hero.

I hope you'll use some of your hero ability to help us here in Appalachia. Maybe you can volunteer here and be a hero of friendship. Maybe you can send a donation and be a hero of generosity. Maybe you can develop new businesses here in Appalachia to help bring economic revival to this troubled region.

Above all, please be a hero of prayer. Pray for us here in Appalachia. We need heroes more than ever before. Pray for our leaders in government, education, and economic development. Pray for the poor and lonely, for those who have no hope, and those who have let despair rule their lives.

Please pray for me. I am constantly aware that my sunset may not be far away. More than ever before I need the prayers and support of my friends far and near. I was greatly strengthened by the many people who sent birthday cards and notes for my 70th birthday in January of 1994. I do not claim to be worthy of the wonderful words contained in these messages, but I hope I can share a few with you anyway, to show how wonderful the people are who share my dream to bring change to Appalachia.

Dear Reverend Beiting,

You have given so much of yourself to the people of Kentucky. What a great example you are to all who want to serve the Lord but think they can't make a difference. Happy Birthday to a very special servant.

Dear Reverend Beiting,

   You have inspired so many of us to share with you in helping in a practical way to make life better for a whole generation of mountain people. The Lord you serve will surely say, ''Well done thy good and faithful servant.'' Your life has been a blessing to all who have been privileged to know you. Many happy returns for the day. May the Lord bless you and grant you many more years. We need you.

Dear Reverend Beiting,

   Please freely receive our thanks as we share in the joy of your seventieth birthday. Your decision to follow Jesus touches many lives—those you see directly and those who are moved to support your work. Thank you for not growing weary of doing the good work you do (though I'm sure you've had struggles over the years). I hope your birthday is filled with laughter and friends.

Dear Reverend Beiting,

Somehow I feel you are my friend even though I don't contribute a lot. I do as I can. I pray for all your people and I want to wish you a very happy, healthy, blessed birthday with many more.

These words of encouragement mean so much to me. I am more excited about life at 70 than I ever was at 26. It is quite possible that the best is yet to come for me and those I love.

For my part, I will try to be faithful. I take my inspiration for faithfulness from an Old Testament hero, Ruth. When Ruth's mother-in-law Naomi decided to return to Israel because her husband and her two sons had all died, Ruth followed her. Naomi asked Ruth why she was following. She said to Ruth "Your husband, my son, is dead. I am destitute and have nothing to offer you. Why do you follow me? Go home to your own people." But Ruth said, "Do not ask me to abandon or forsake you! For wherever you go I will go, wherever you lodge I will lodge, your people shall be my people, and your God my God. Wherever you die I will die, and there be buried."

This is my pledge of faithfulness to the CAP family, including all those who give their time, money, and prayers to support our work. I care about you, I worry about you, I pray for you every

day. Wherever you go, I go with you in spirit.
Your people are my people. Your God is my God.

I hope that someday, when our lives are over,
we can live together where the sun shines on a new
frontier of the heart.

Reverend Beiting, the Hero

Reverend Beiting loves to talk about his favorite hero, Daniel Boone. But to many of us who work with him each day, Reverend Beiting is the real hero. He is the one who overcomes enormous obstacles to lead people to their dreams. Through his example and his vision, he not only helps the poor of Appalachia, he also inspires every person who has the unique opportunity to know him.

This past January, Reverend Beiting turned 70 years old. As the President of the Christian Appalachian Project, I have the difficult task of trying to fill his shoes as age slows him down. Luckily, it has not yet slowed him much. Though I feel up to the task of carrying on the practical work of directing this wonderful organization, I will need the help of all of Reverend Beiting's friends far and near if I am ever to carry on his dream to open a new frontier.

Thankfully, Reverend Beiting has always attracted the most remarkable people to his side, and the Christian Appalachian Project is blessed with these people as employees, volunteers, and donors.

Two of them took the writing of this book, and the occasion of his 70th birthday to put down their thoughts about Reverend Beiting, the hero.

Mike McLaughlin
CAP President

Ed Riley (CAP volunteer)

When I was a child, my heroes were of a fantasy world—men and women who could leap tall buildings with a single bound, stop speeding trains, and thwart evil wherever it lurked. As I grew older, these heroes were replaced by heroes of the real world—men and women who had great wealth, popularity, or power. It wasn't until I came to work for the Christian Appalachian Project that I finally realized that the real heroes are the heroes of God's Kingdom.

Reverend Beiting is that kind of hero.

I admire him and look up to him as an example for my own life. I know he is that same kind of example for thousands of people throughout the mountains of Appalachia and here at CAP.

Reverend Beiting lives his strong faith in Jesus. His courage and convictions have persevered through 45 years of daily challenges. I have seen him beg for food for the poor, labor to build houses for the homeless, wade through floods to reach the sick, and travel thousands of miles every year to share the gospel story.

Wherever I go in Appalachia I hear people talk about "the Catholic priest who never gives up, says no . . . who is always there."

One of the things I find most inspiring about Reverend Beiting is that he truly lives a life of prayer. He begins his day with prayer. He prays throughout the day. I can't remember how many times we have prayed while driving in a car to visit some new project or to solve some crisis. No matter how tired he is at the end of a long day, he never fails to remember in prayer all those who have come into his life that day.

Many of his everyday sacrifices go unnoticed by all but those of us who work closely with him. He suffers from diabetes, cataracts, and various disabilities caused by several auto accidents. A few days ago he was excitedly discussing his dream to create jobs by starting two new businesses. As he spoke, he tried to raise his ailing right leg over a roll of carpet at his feet. After fifteen seconds of trying and failing, he simply reached over and lifted his leg with his hand and placed it over the carpet, without once letting up in describing his dream. I know he was in pain, but he never said a word. With all his health problems, he can still outwork two people half his age.

Working with Reverend Beiting is a pleasure and a treasure I will never forget. Because of him, I finally know what a true flesh-and-blood hero is.

In closing, I offer an old prayer:

> God, will You go before him, to guide him
> and show him the way. And will You come
> behind him to watch over him and protect
> him from every harm and danger. And God,
> will You hover above him and shower down
> on him every blessing and grace. But most
> of all Lord, will You come and dwell within
> him and be his friend for always.

Kathleen Leavell (CAP employee and
former volunteer)

Writing about my hero, Reverend Beiting, is a
humbling task. I don't think a day goes by that
I don't use a gift that was either given by, or nur-
tured by, him.

One of the first things that comes to my mind
in describing Reverend Beiting is his commitment.
Forty-five years in the mountains is a long time.
When I worked with him, there never seemed to
be time to celebrate one victory before another
need arose. For every solution there were another
dozen problems; always another child without
glasses, another family without food, another
father without work. Whenever I felt overwhelmed, Reverend Beiting's example of commitment and perseverance would inspire me to go on.
He often reminded me of Mother Teresa's words,
''We are not called to be successful, we are called

to be faithful.''

I remember very clearly a day when it was brought home to me what Reverend Beiting's commitment means to the people of Appalachia. Reverend Beiting and I were standing on the side of a hill surveying one of his new projects. As we stood there, a pickup truck stopped and a woman leaned out the window and shouted, ''Are you the preacher's gonna build us a school?'' I don't even remember what Reverend Beiting said. What I do remember is the woman's eyes. I said to myself, ''So that's what hope looks like.''

I carry the lessons I learned from Reverend Beiting wherever I go. He is a model of faith and a symbol of hope. I draw from these gifts every day and I never feel more fulfilled than when I believe I am passing Reverend Beiting's lessons on to my children.

Thank you Reverend Beiting.

THE MOUNTAIN SPIRIT

Our bimonthly magazine, *The Mountain Spirit,* will keep you up-to-date on the work of the Christian Appalachian Project as we continue to help the people of this poverty-stricken area help themselves. In the magazine, you will also find moving, inspiring stories about the people we serve. If you would like to subscribe to this publication (or renew your subscription), please complete the order form below.

_____

THE MOUNTAIN SPIRIT Subscription Order Form

Please enter my one-year subscription to *The Mountain Spirit.* I have enclosed my check for $6.00, made payable to CAP.

Name _____

Address_____

City _____ State _____ Zip _____

Please return this Order Form, along with your check, to: Christian Appalachian Project, 322 Crab Orchard Road, Lancaster, KY 40446-0001.

_____

Volunteering With
THE CHRISTIAN APPALACHIAN PROJECT:

☐ I am interested in volunteering for one year.
  Please send information.

Name _____

Address_____

City _____ State _____ Zip _____

Please return this form to: Christian Appalachian Project, 322 Crab Orchard Road, Lancaster, KY 40446-0001, (606) 792-2219.

If You'd Like to
Know More About the
Christian Appalachian Project . . .

For more information about CAP, or for
additional copies of *Frontier of the Heart*,
please write or phone us at our headquarters:

Christian Appalachian Project
322 Crab Orchard Road
Lancaster, KY 40446-0001
(606) 792-3051

Thank you for your interest and support!